12

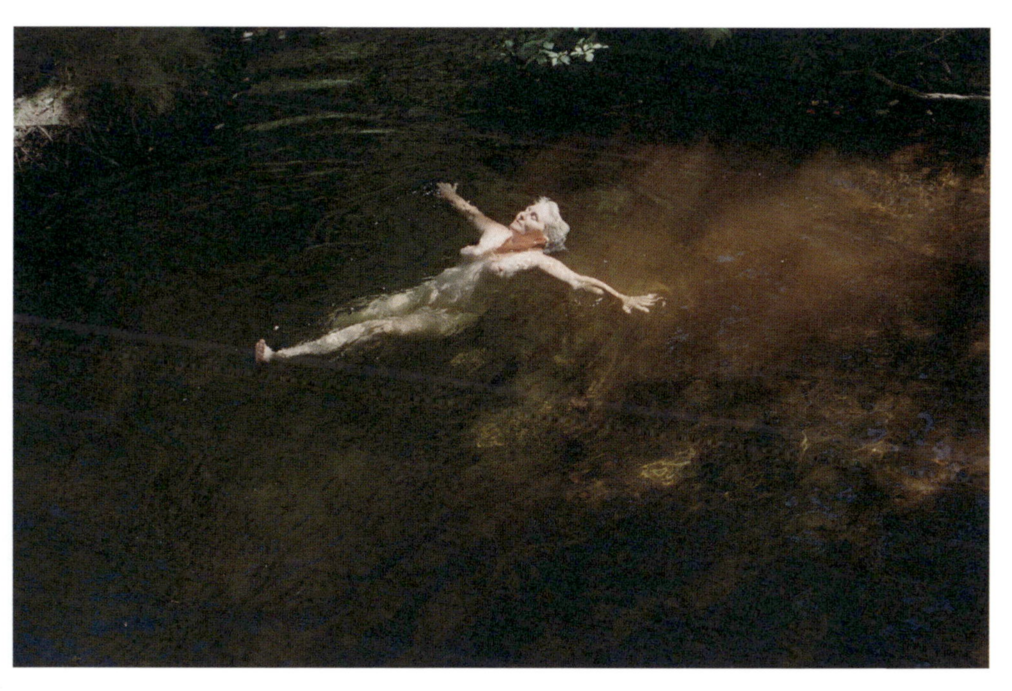

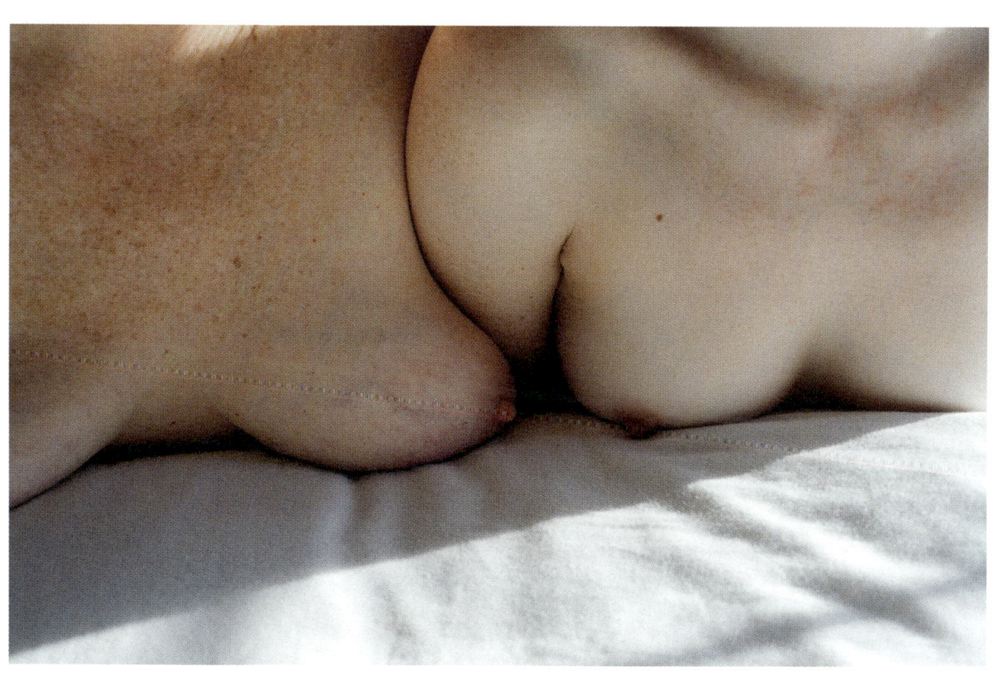

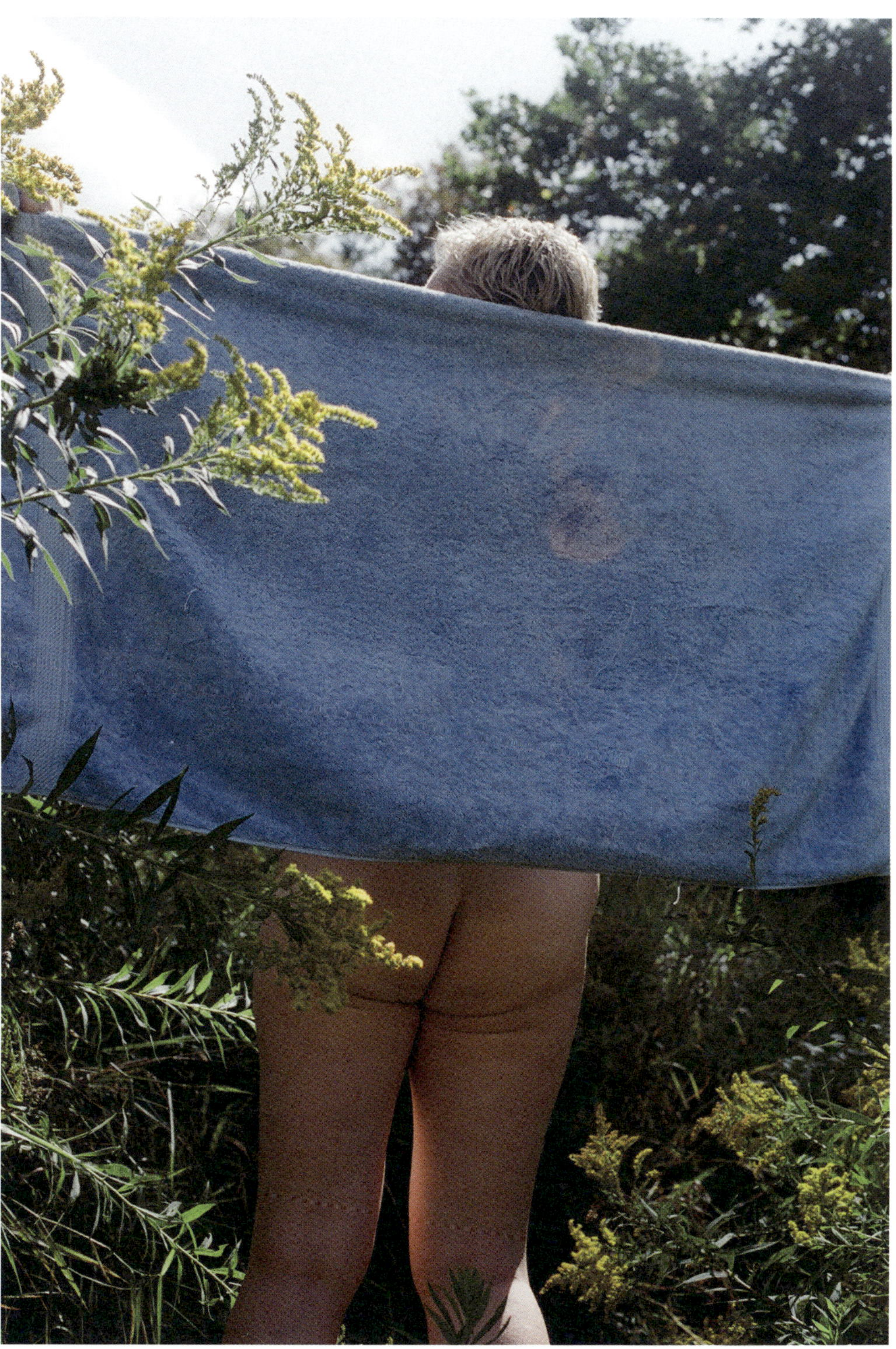

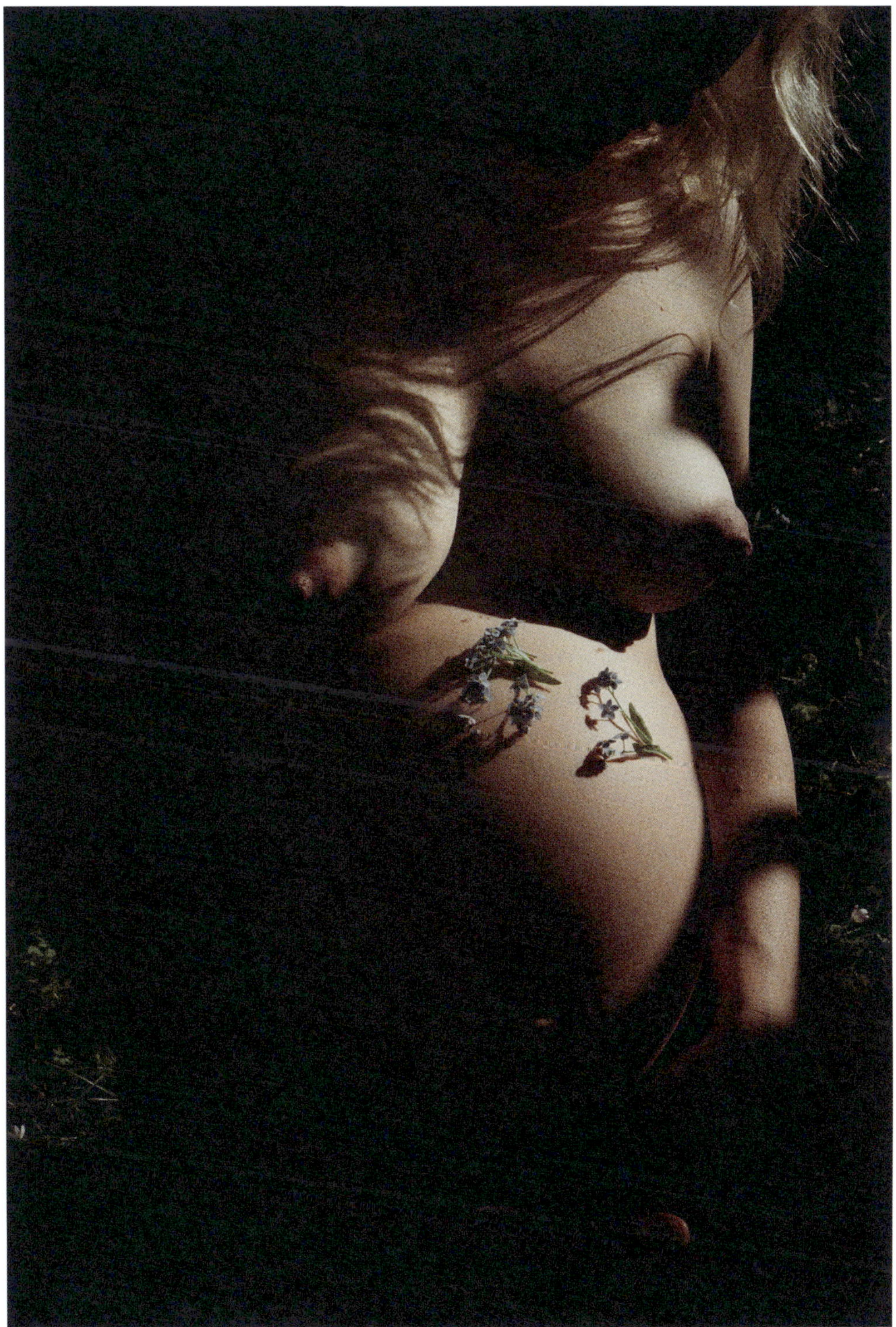

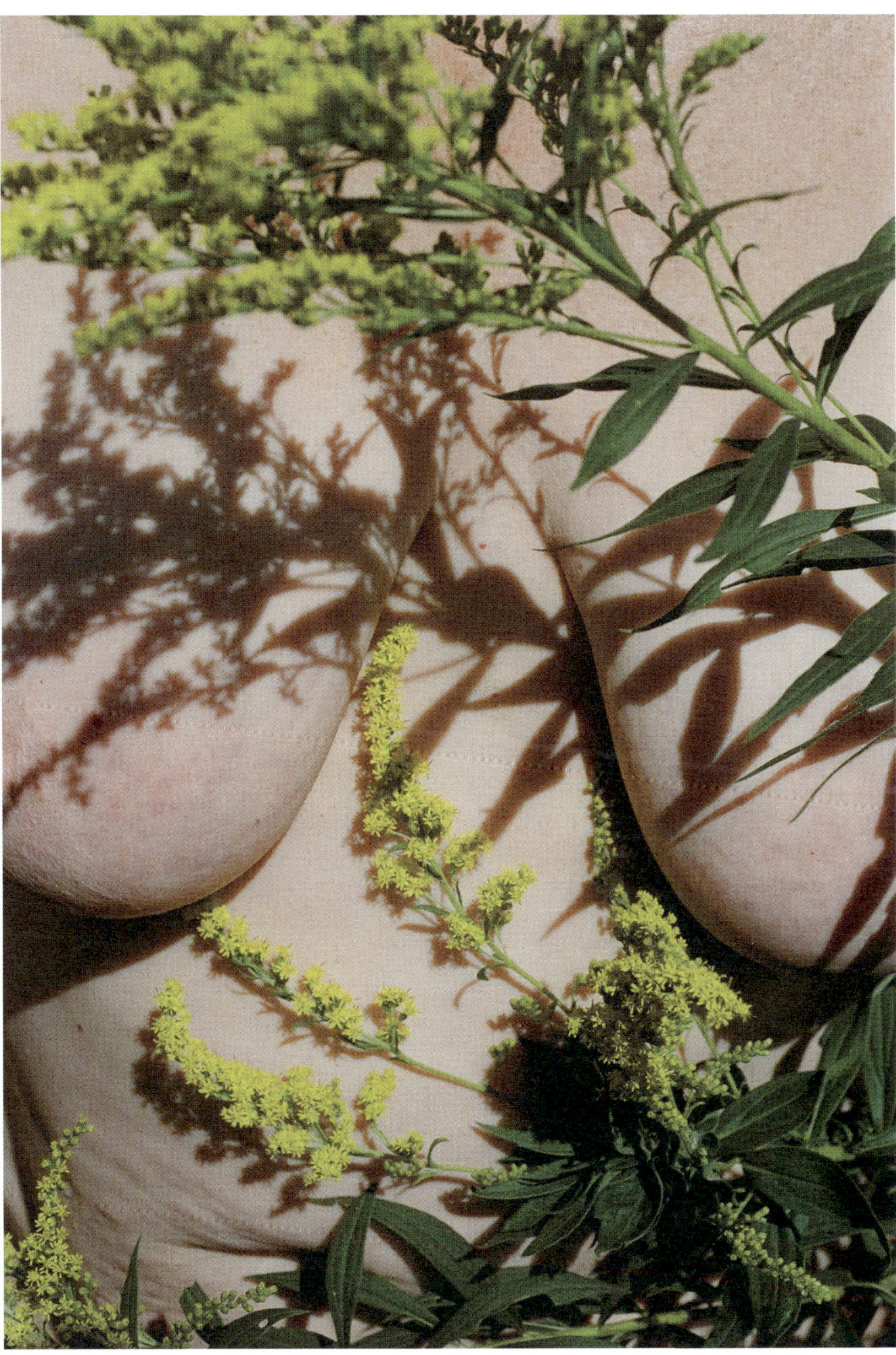

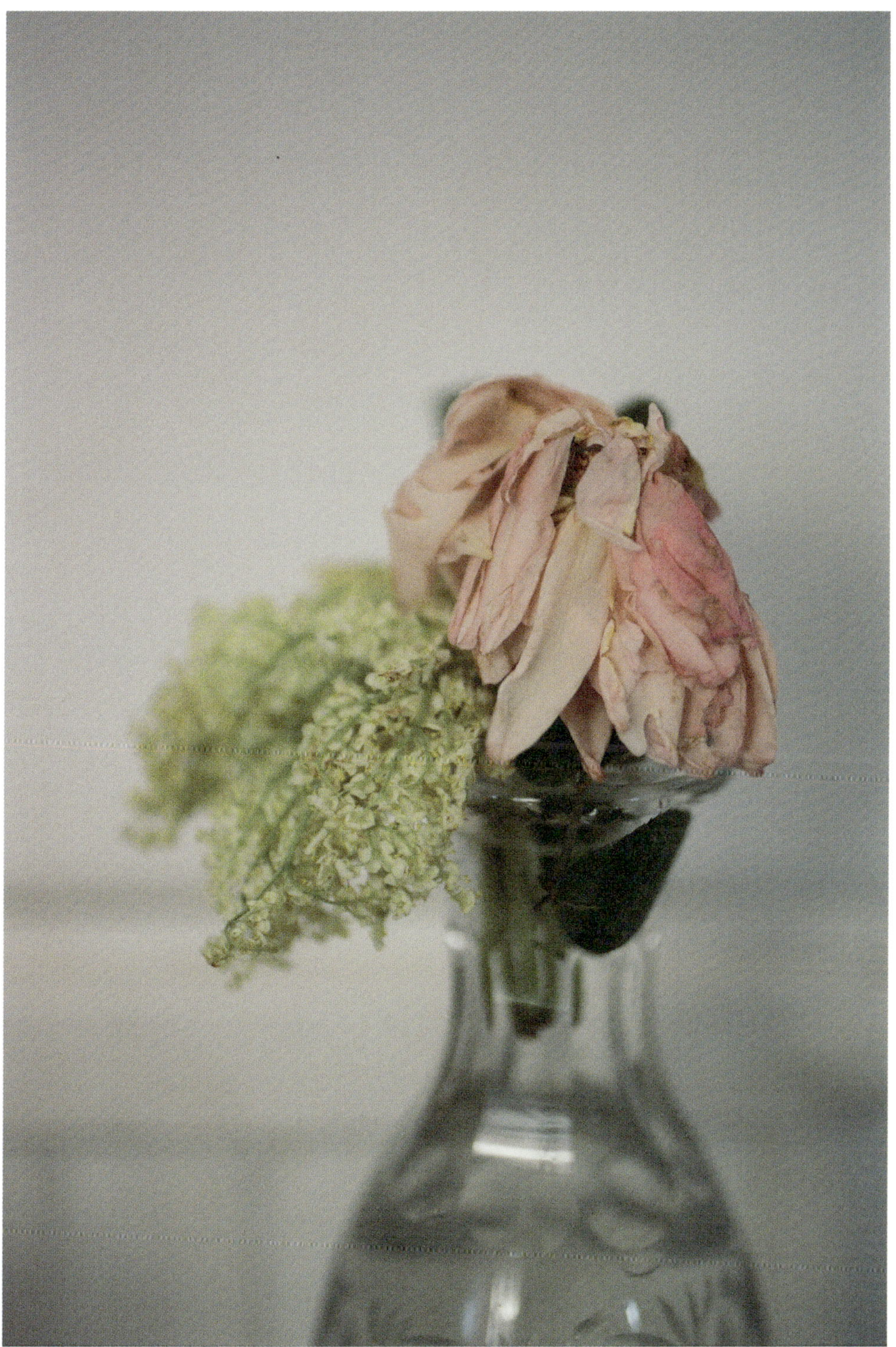

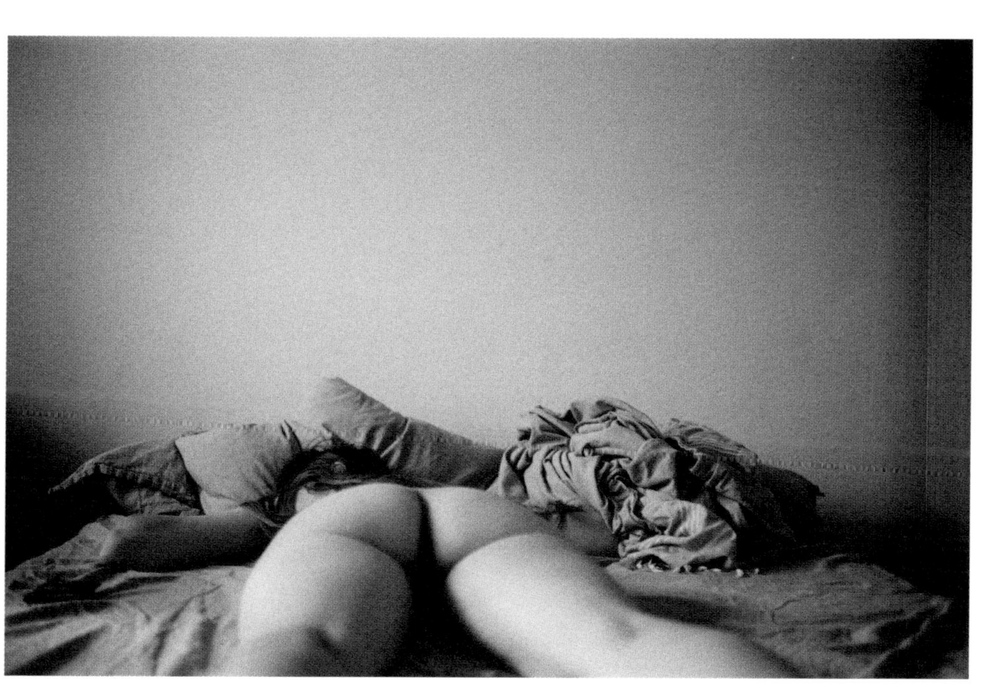

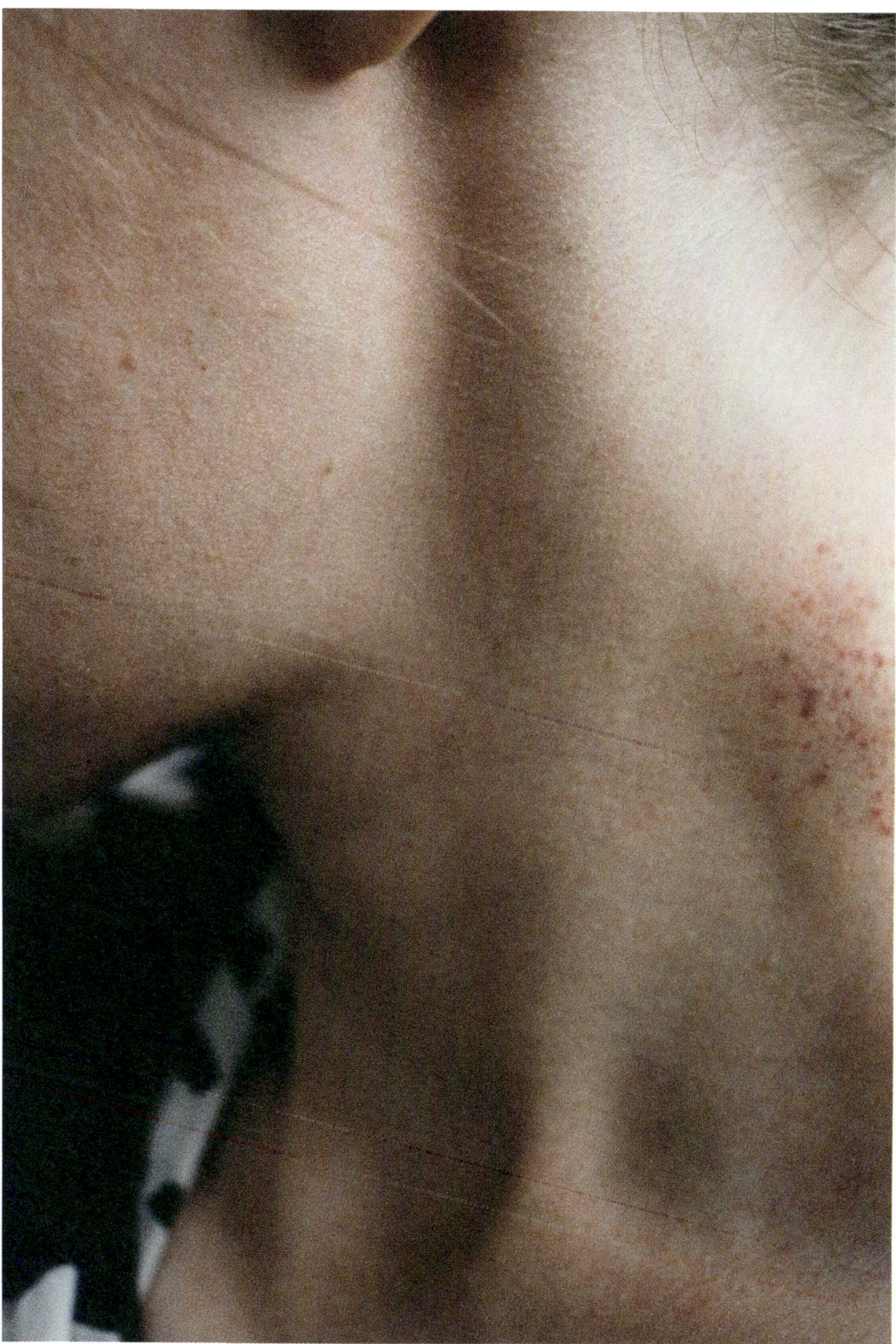

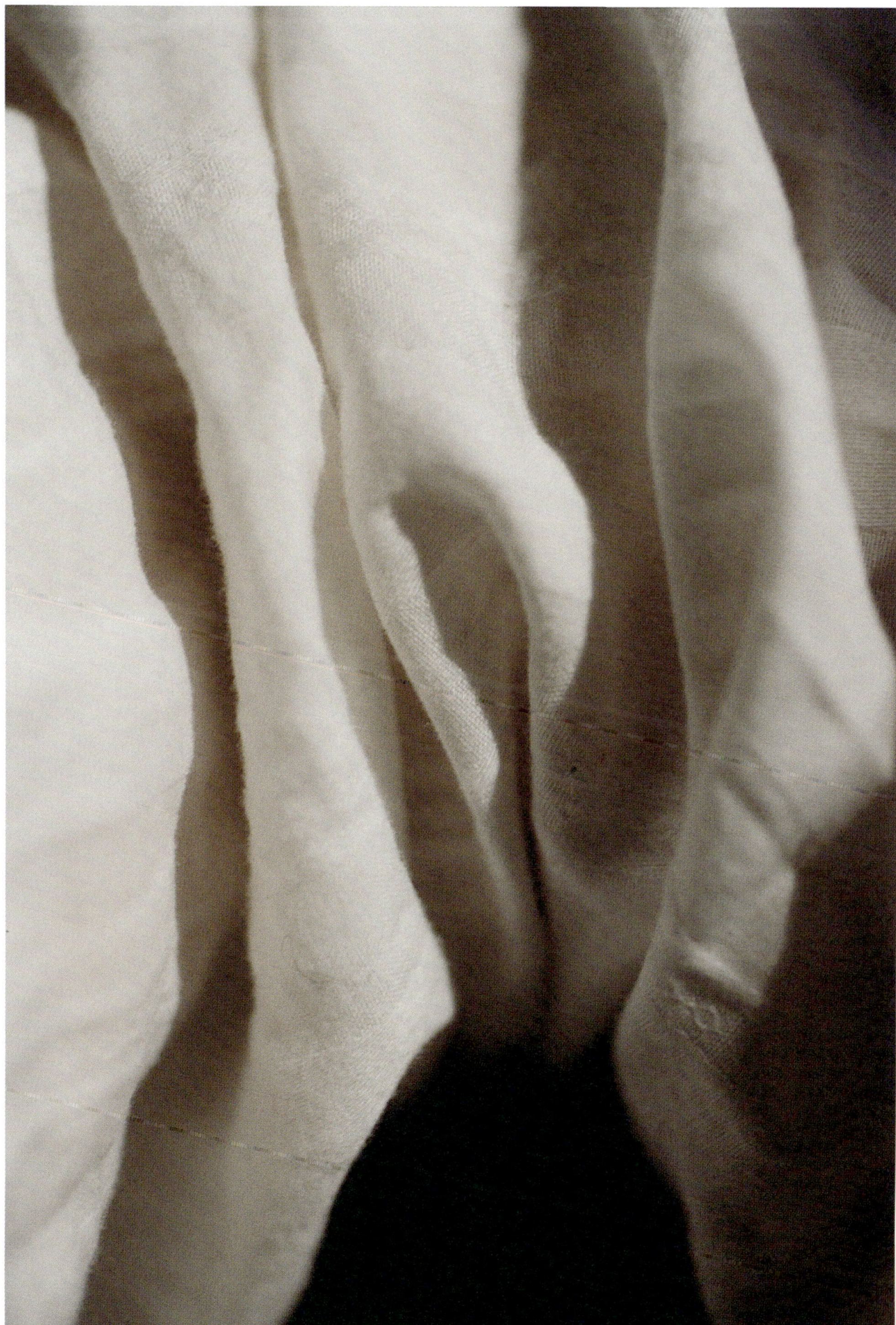

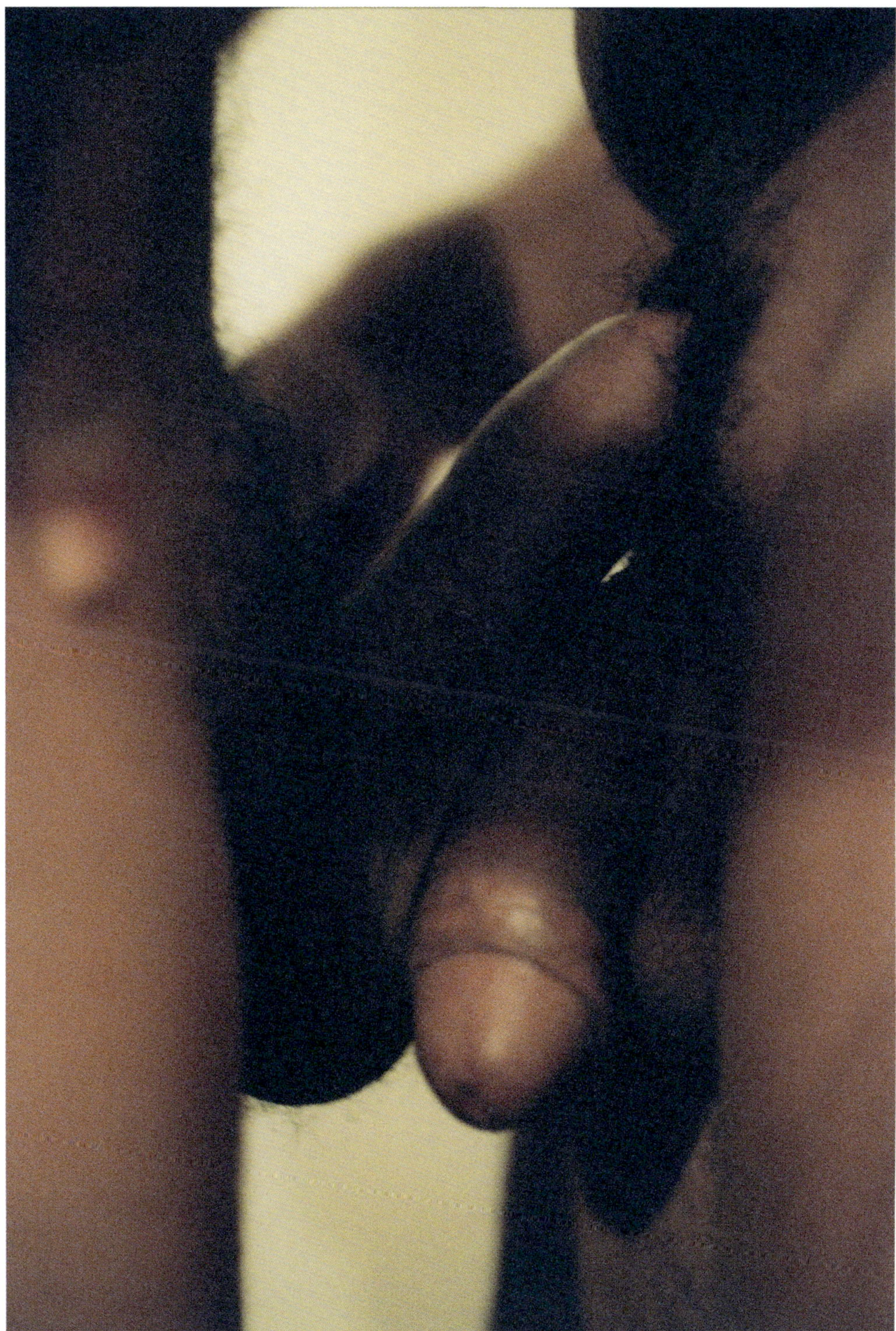

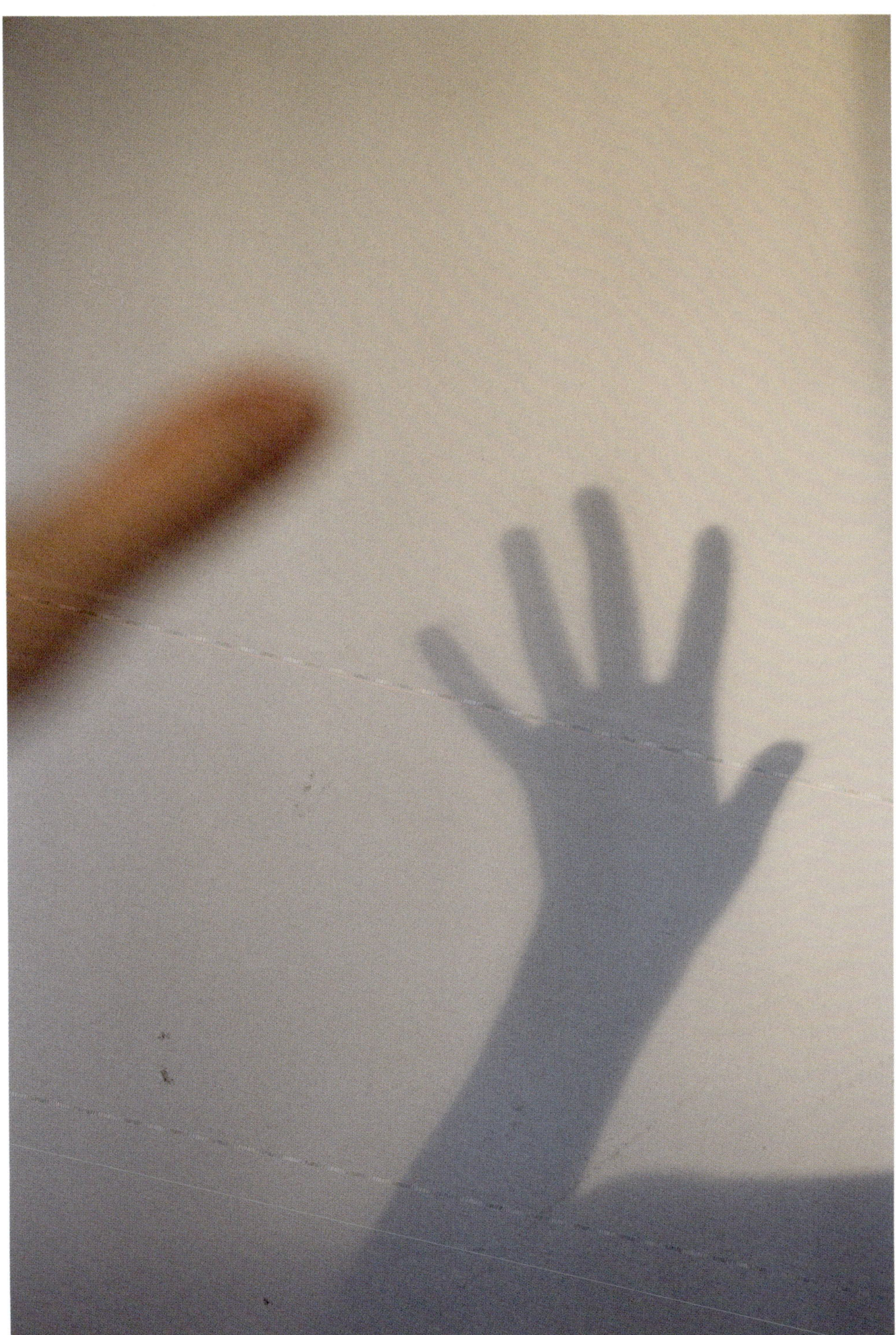

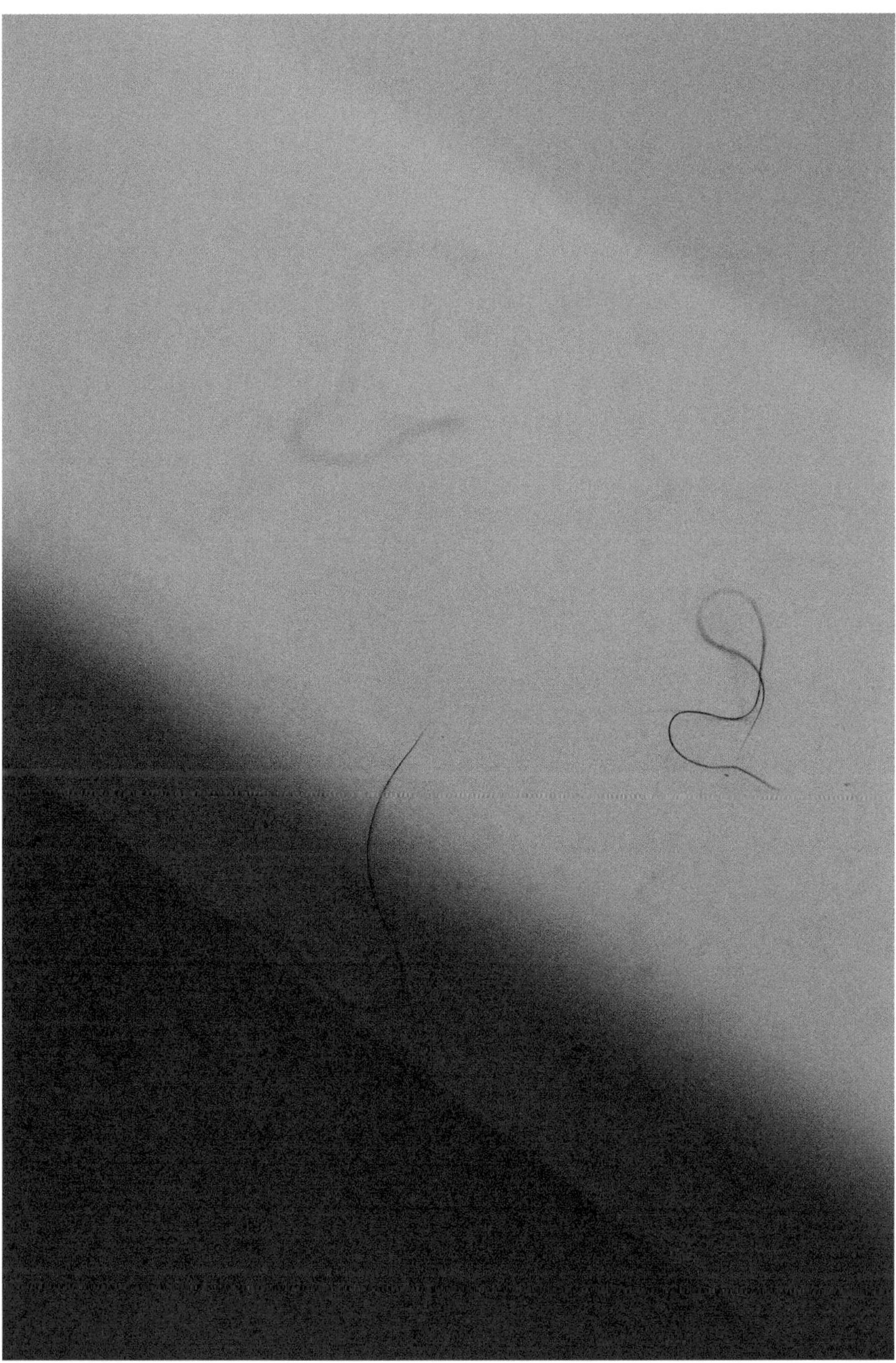

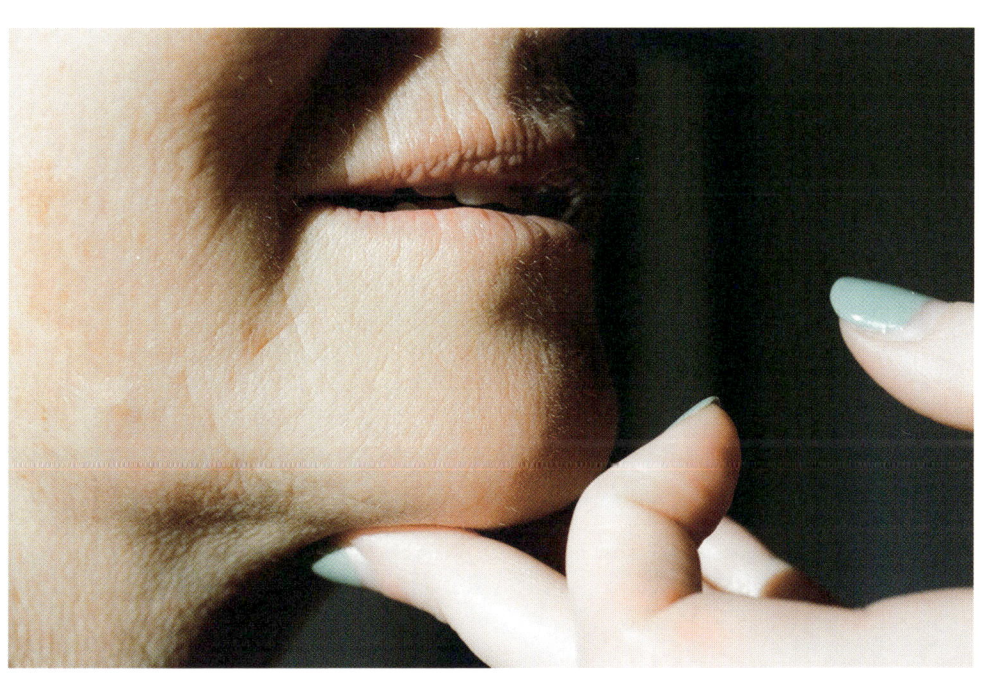

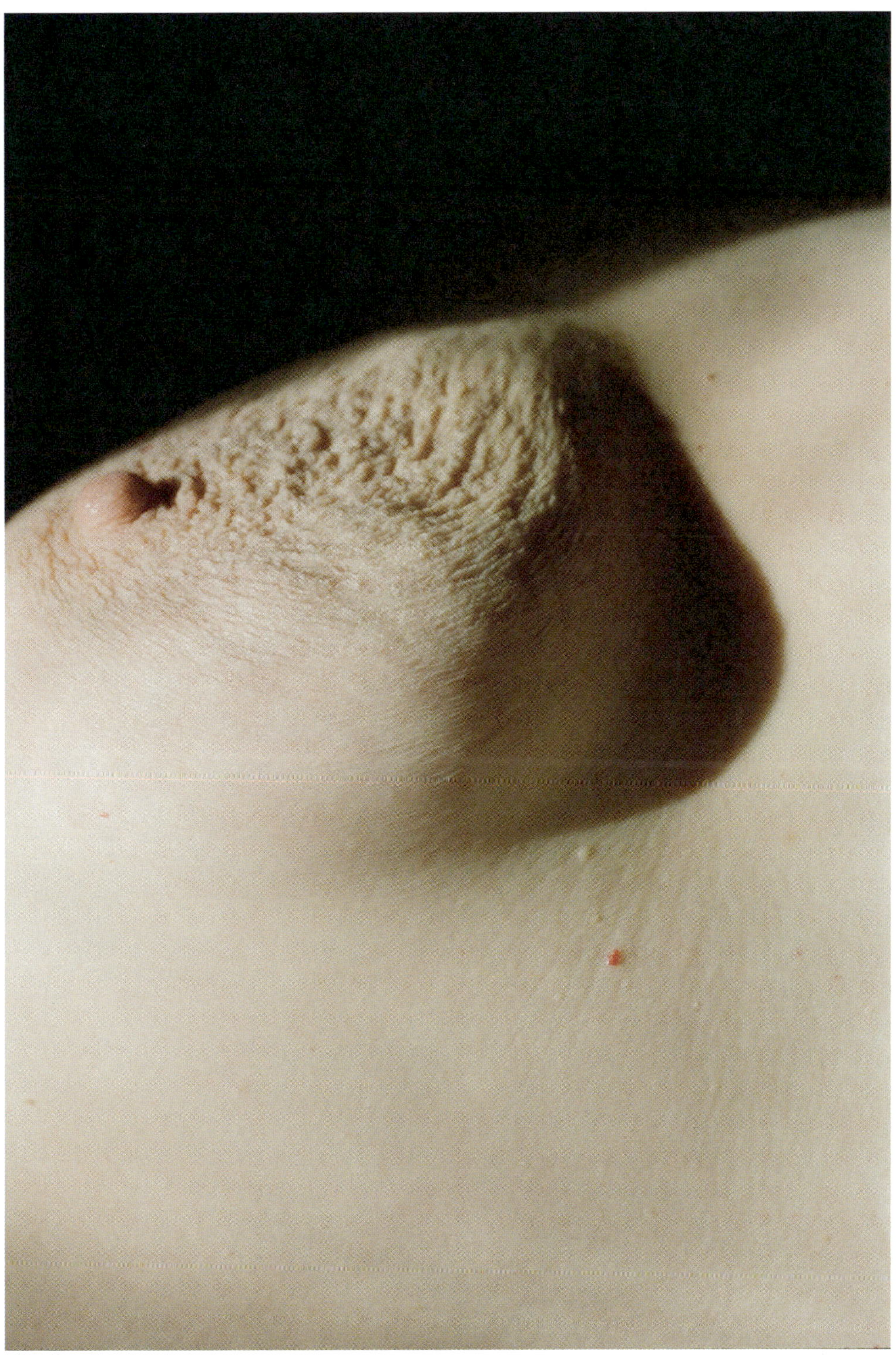

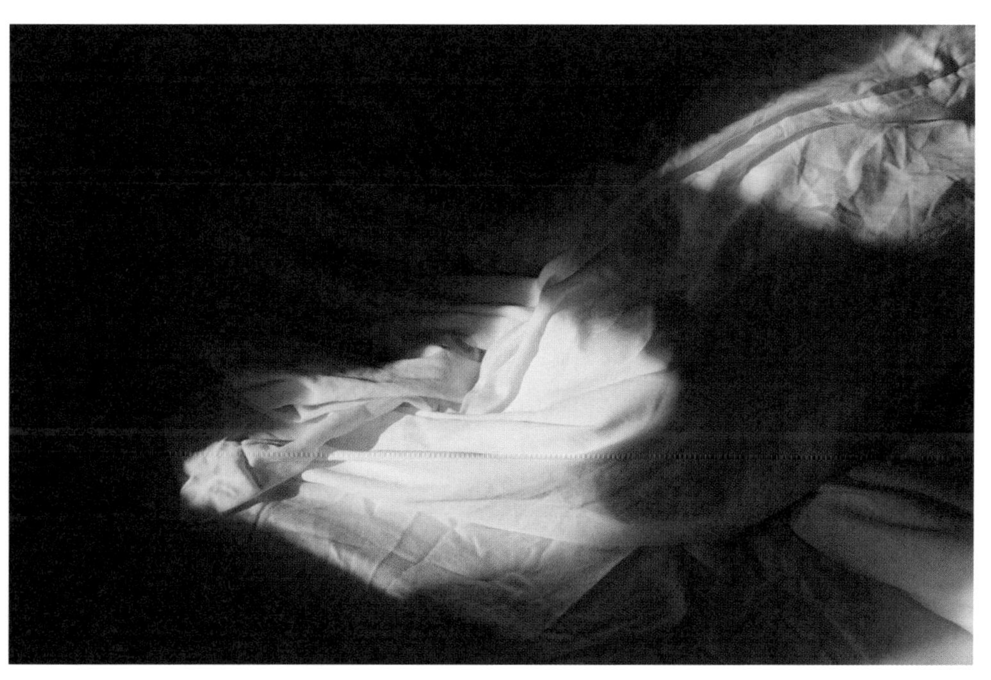

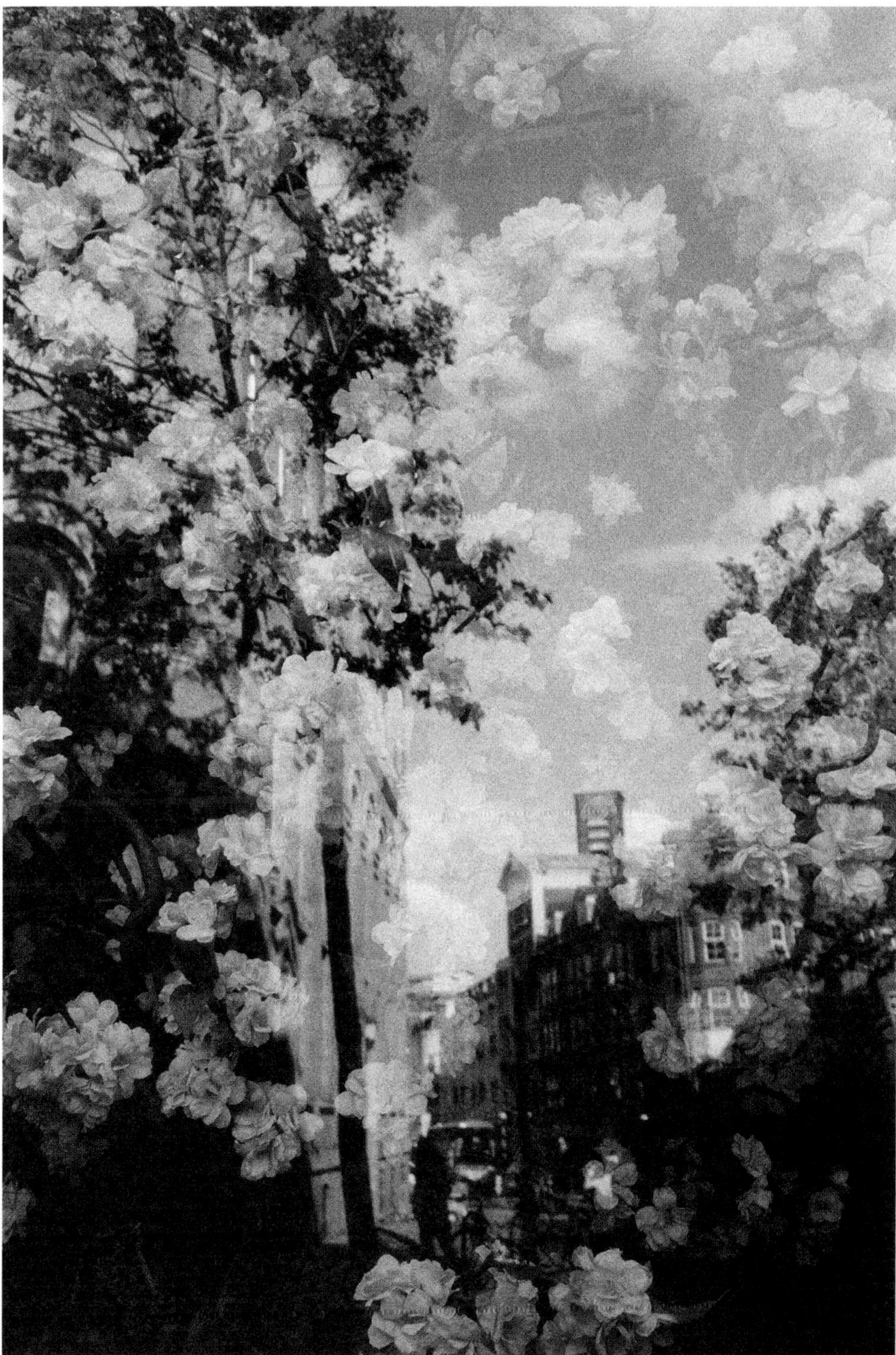

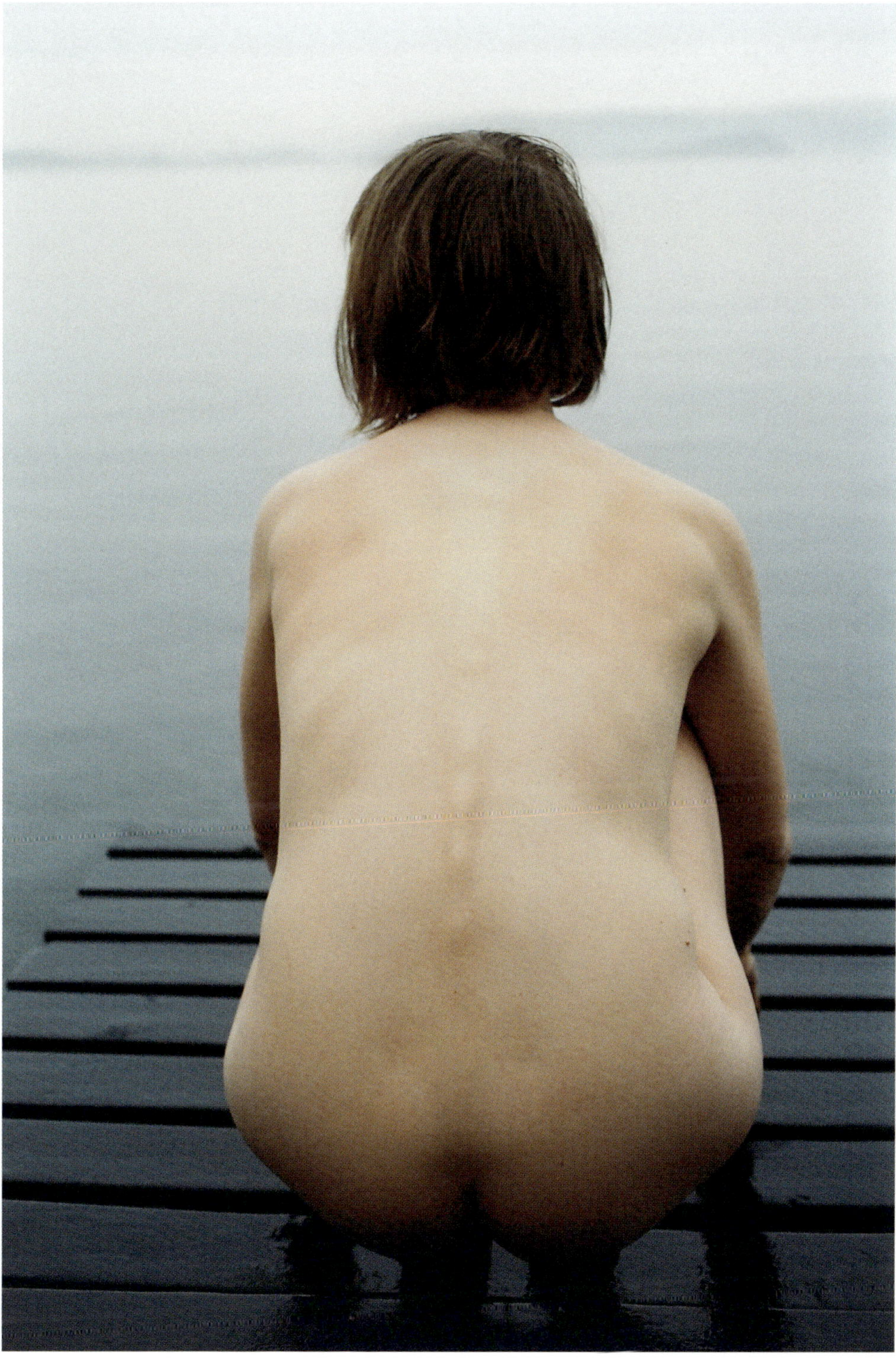

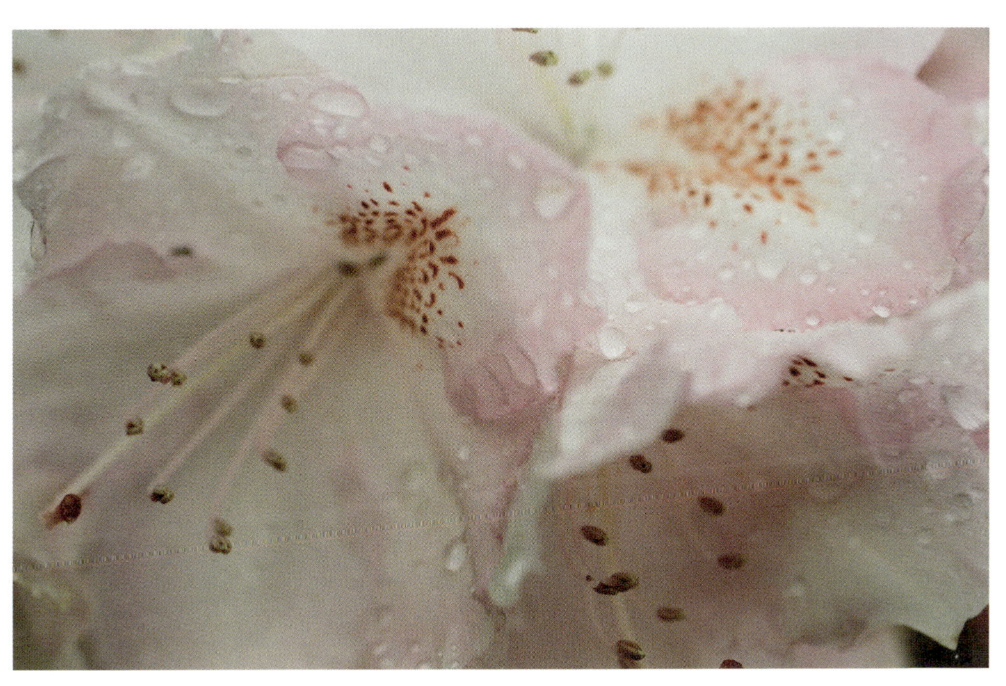

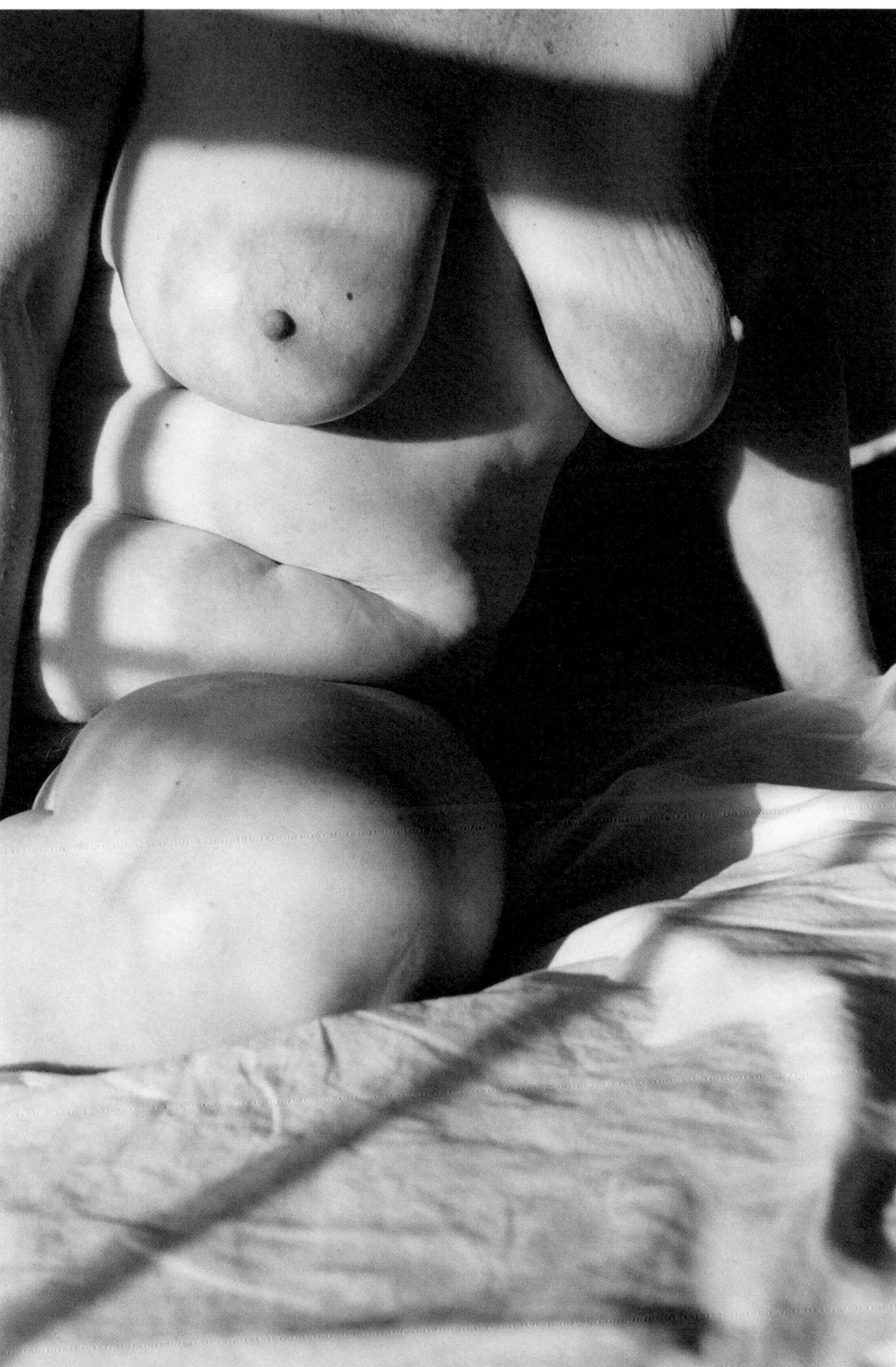

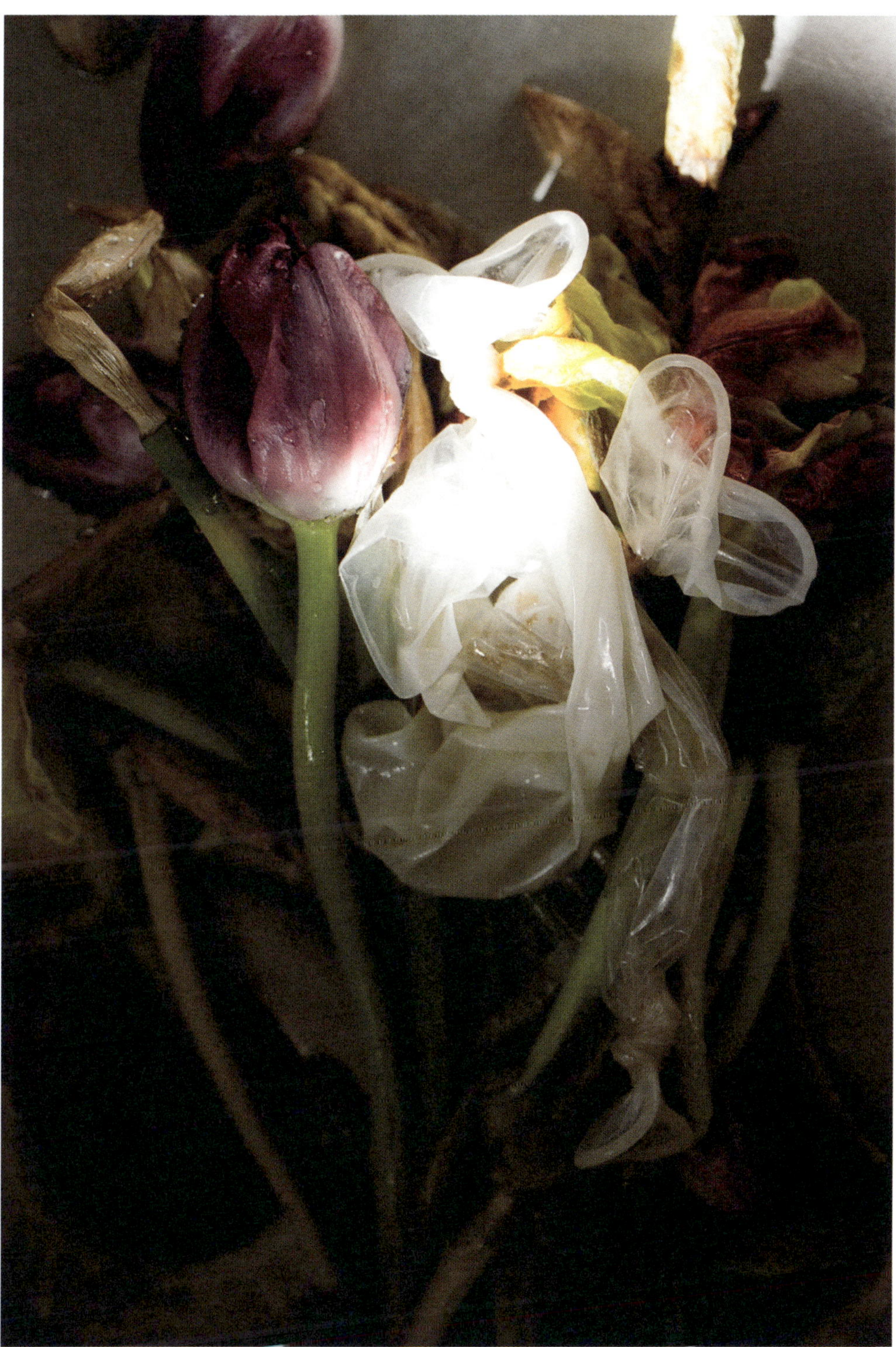

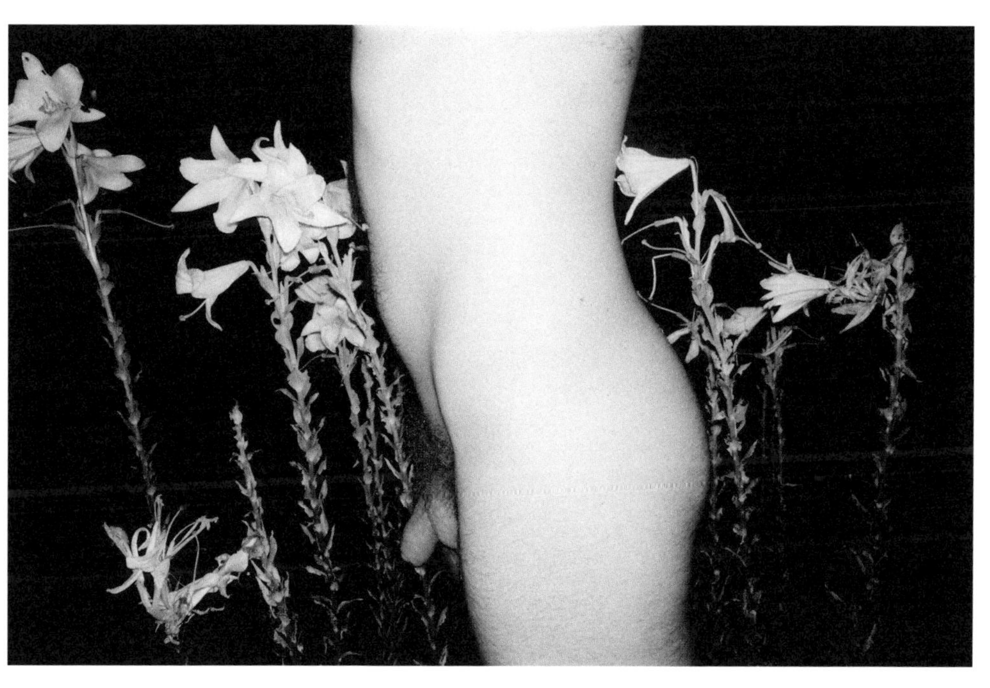

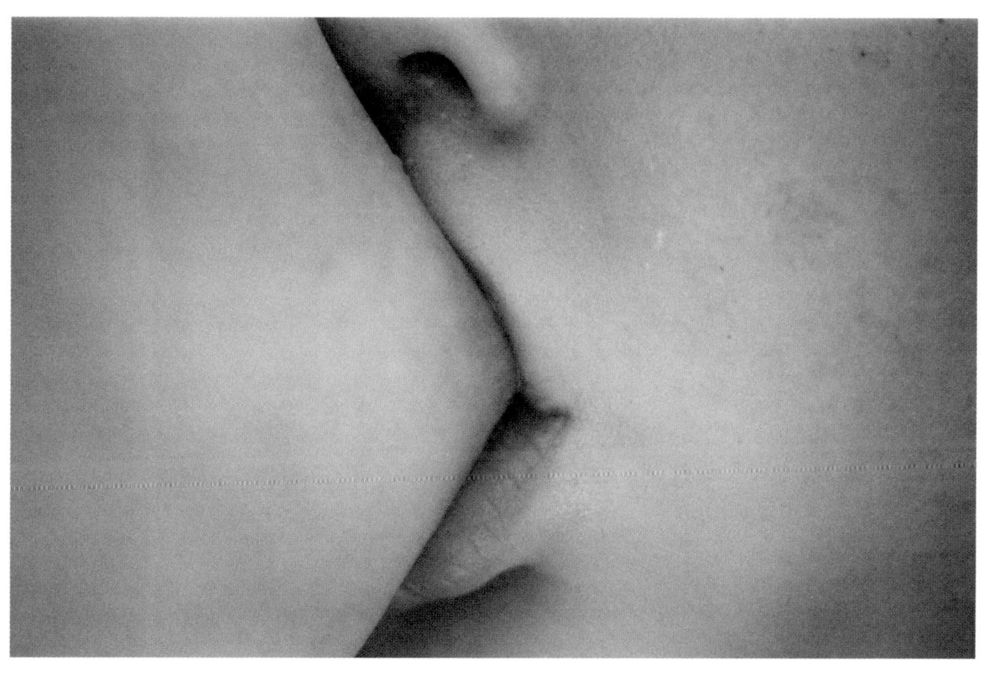

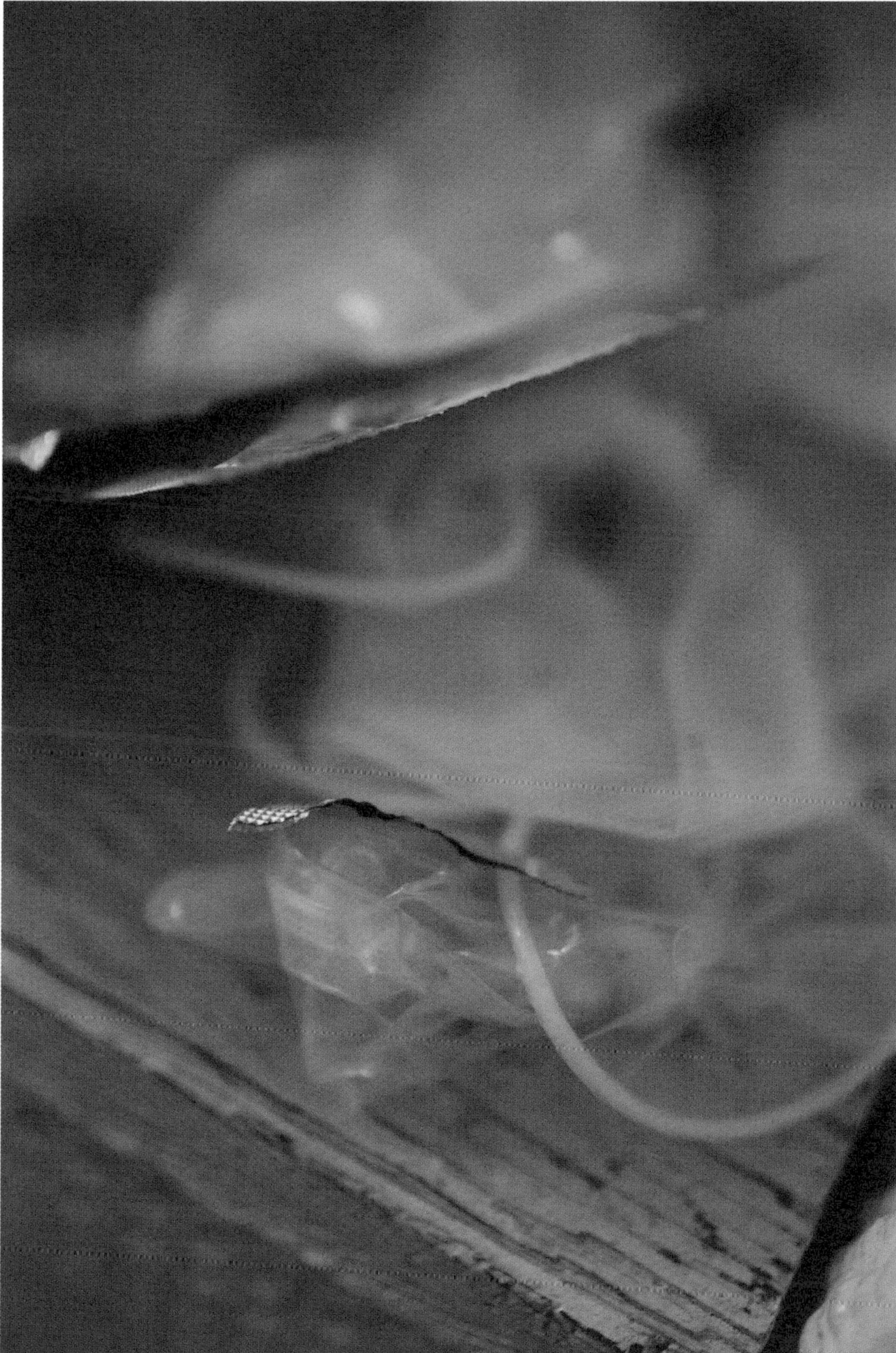

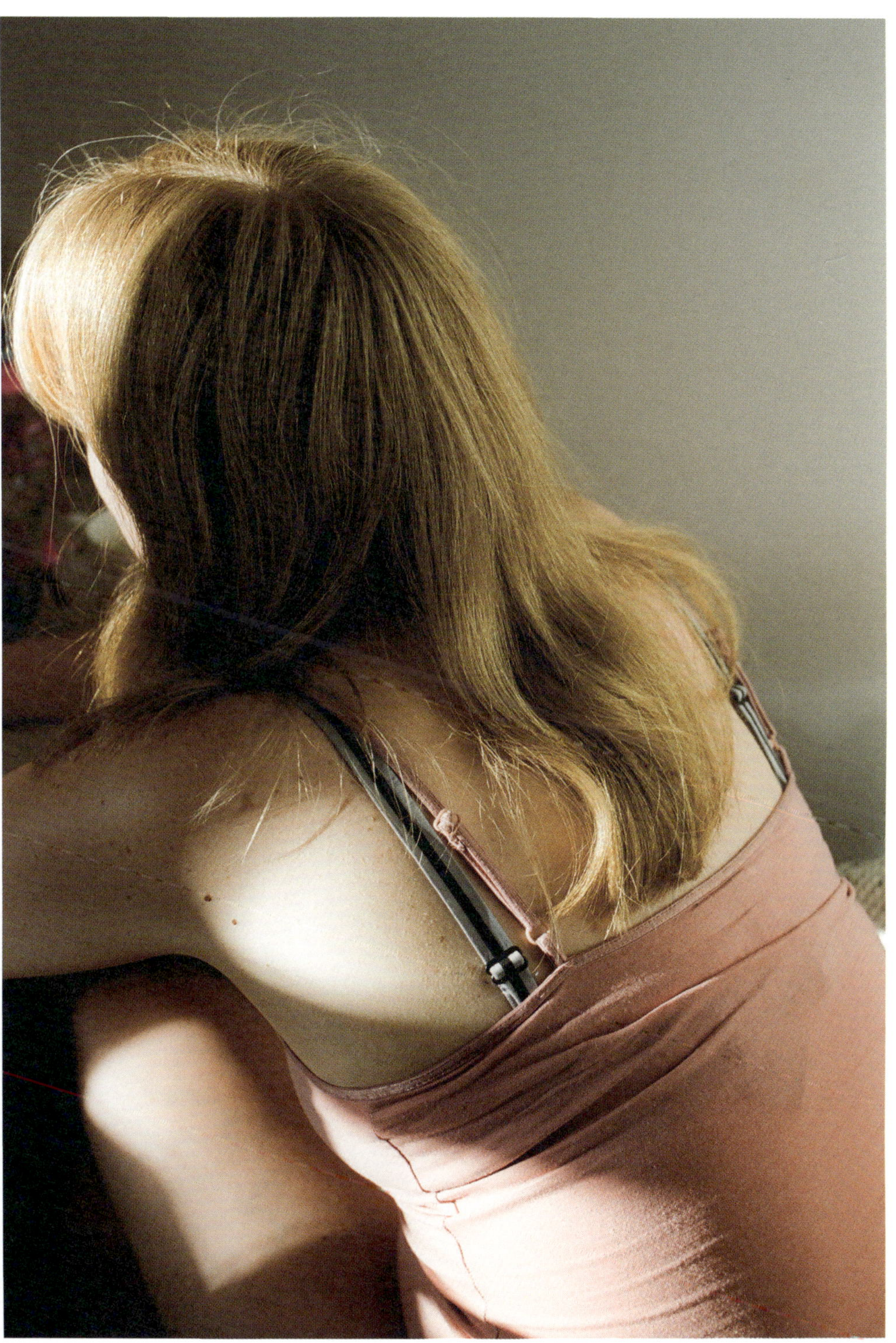

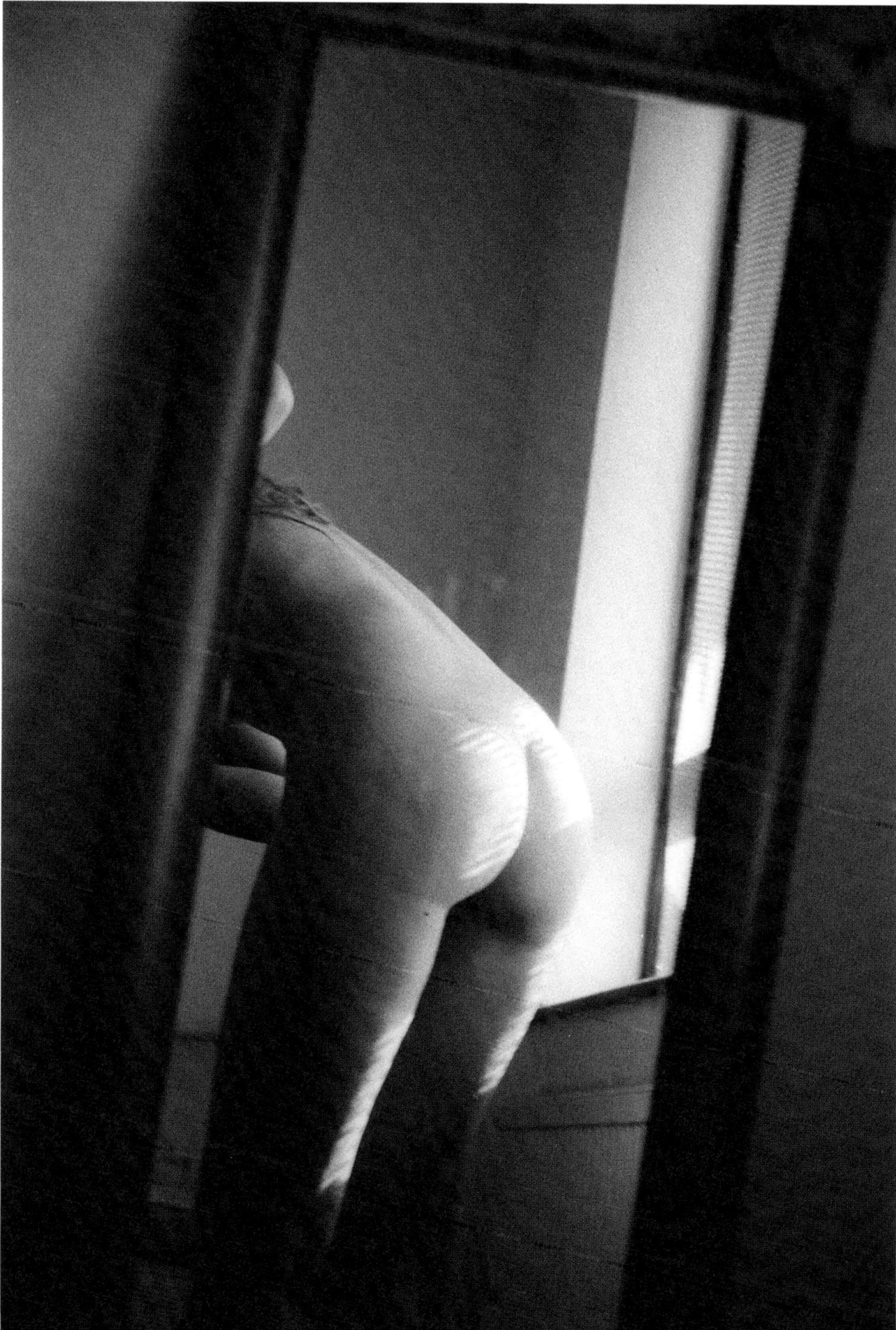

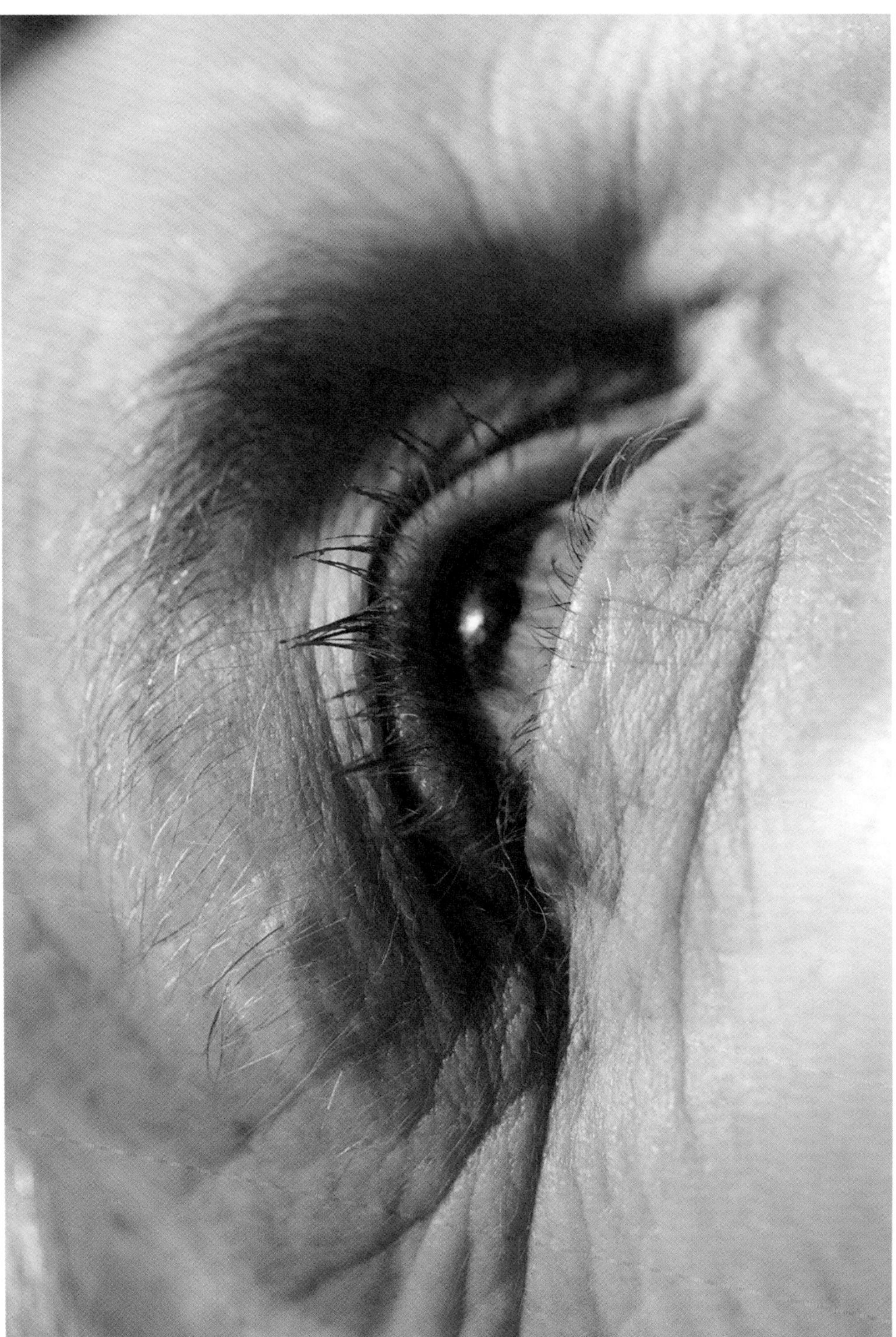

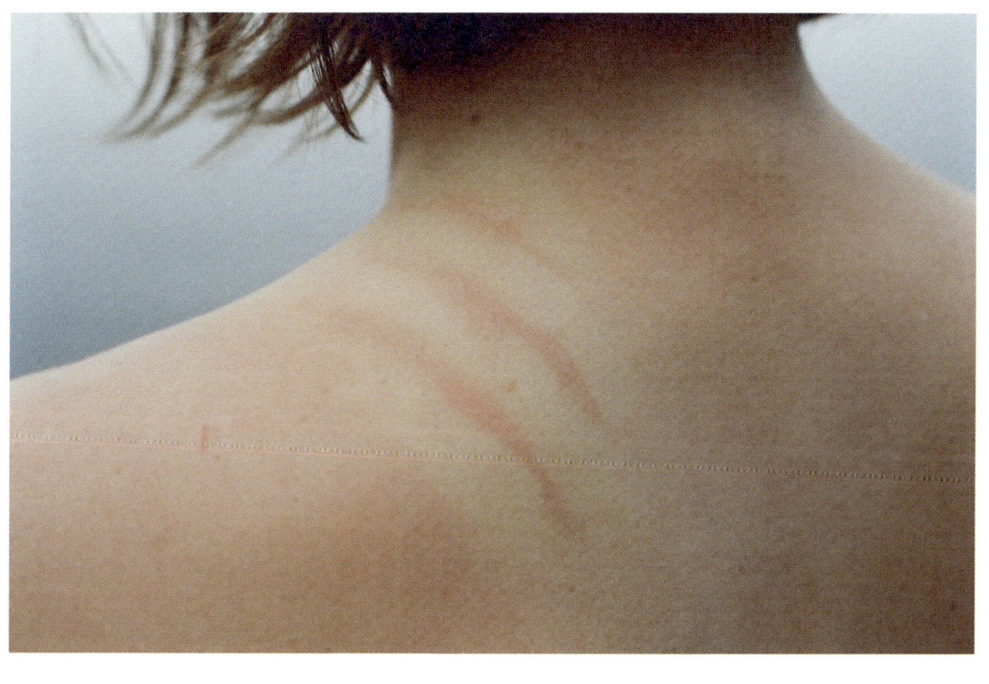

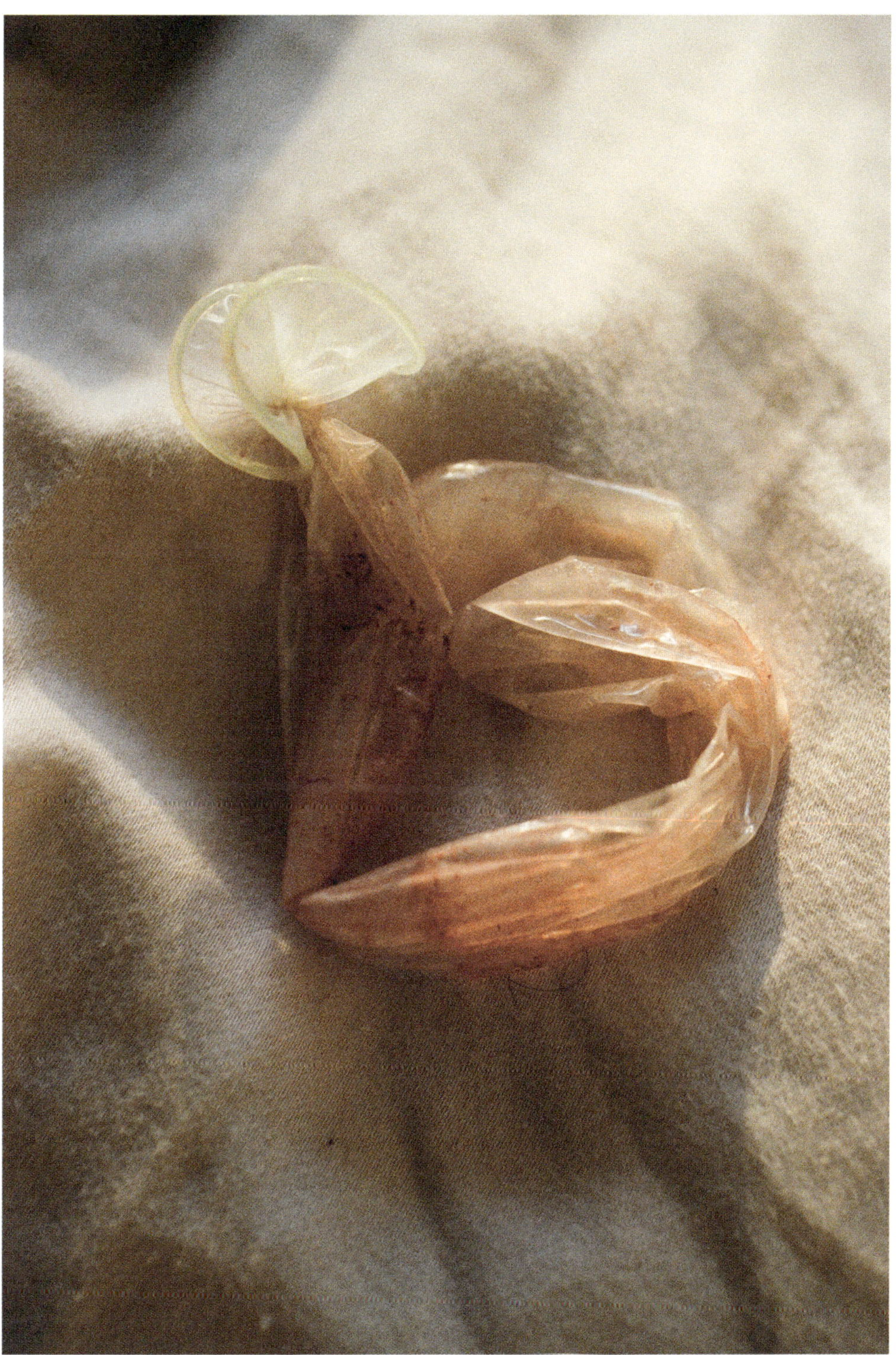

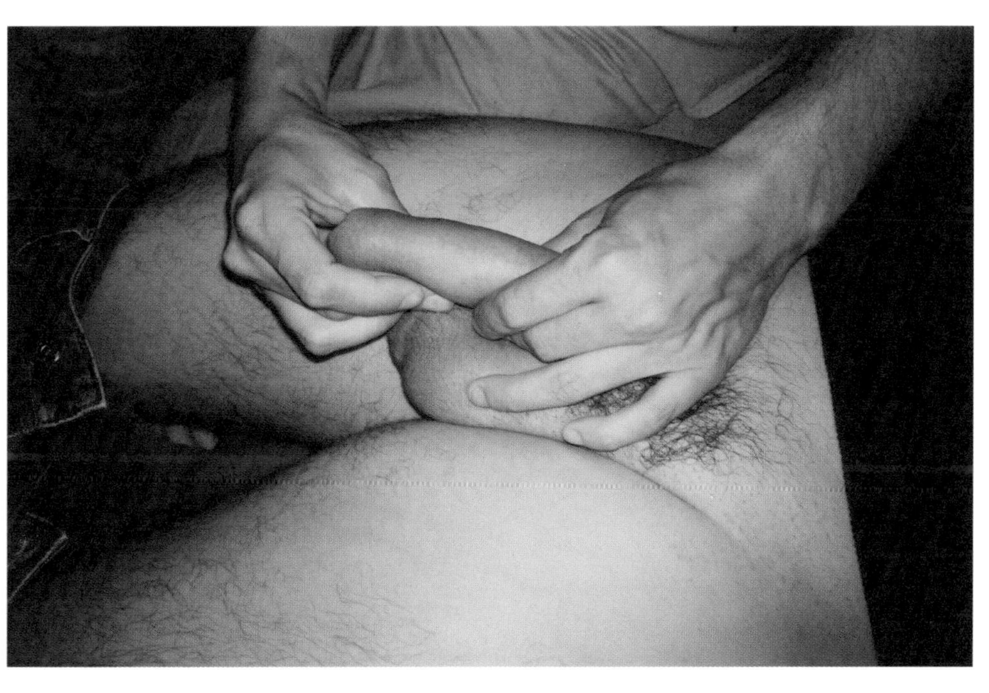

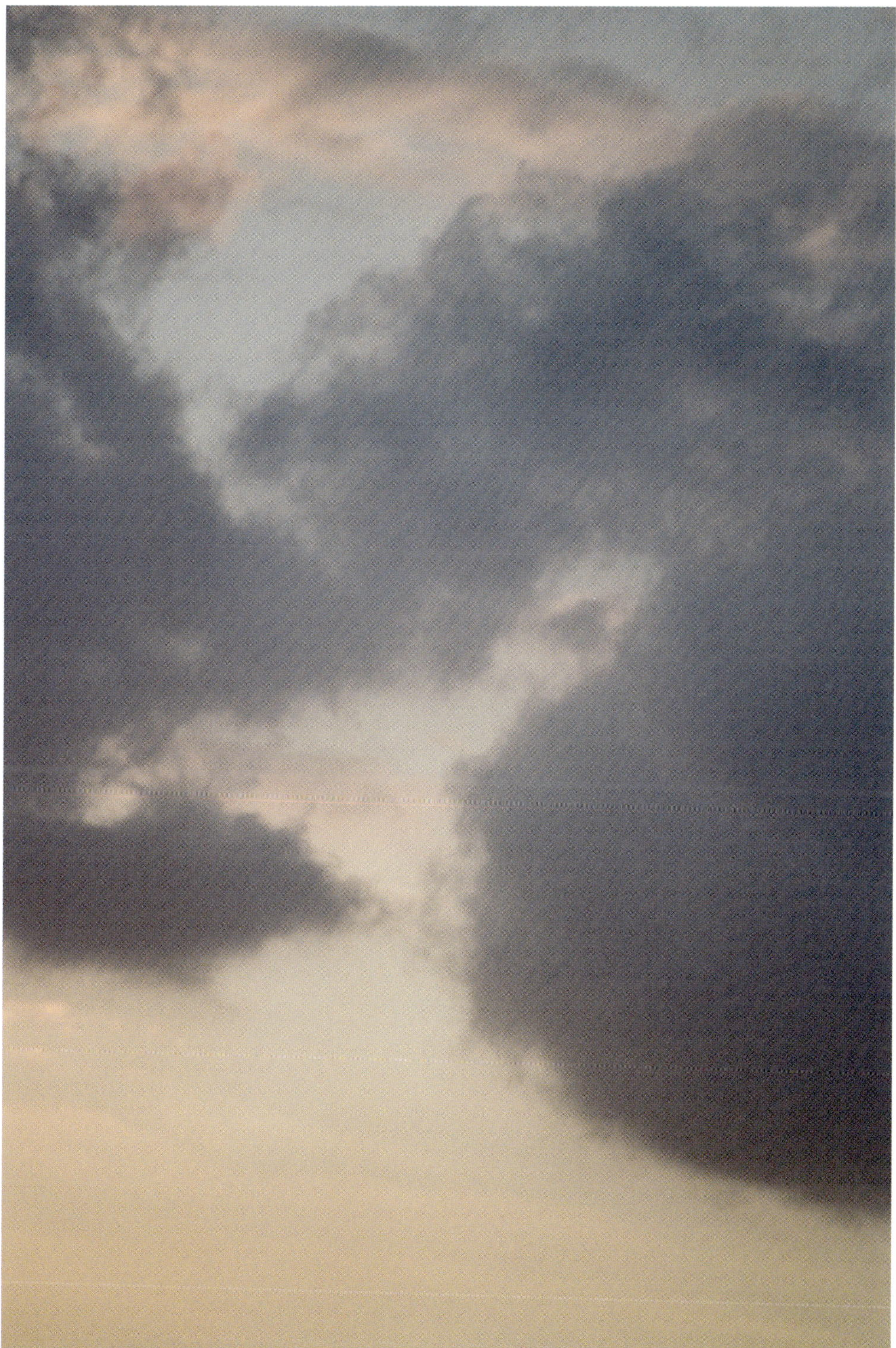

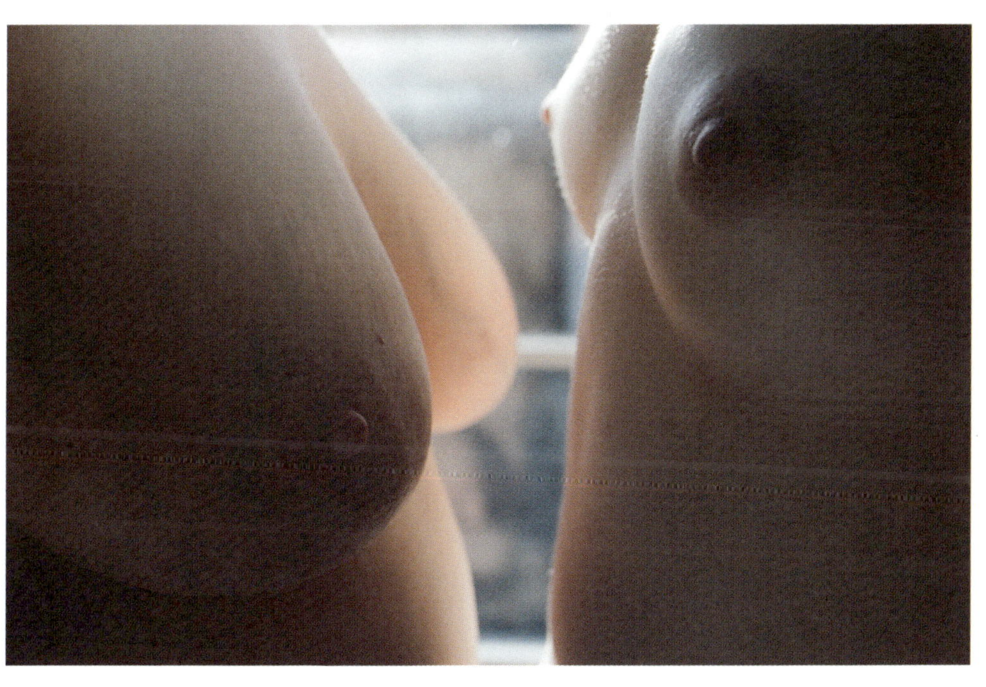

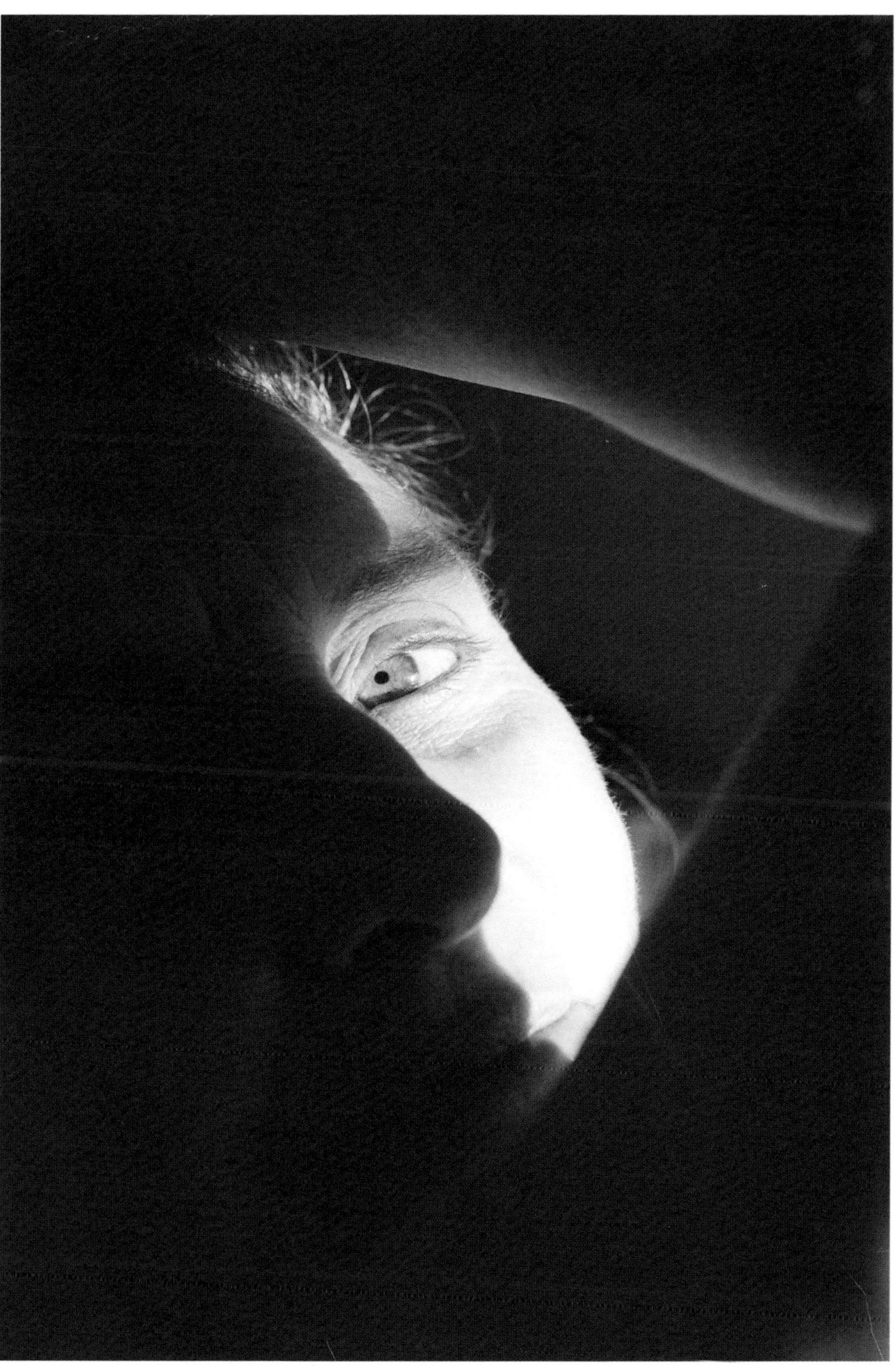

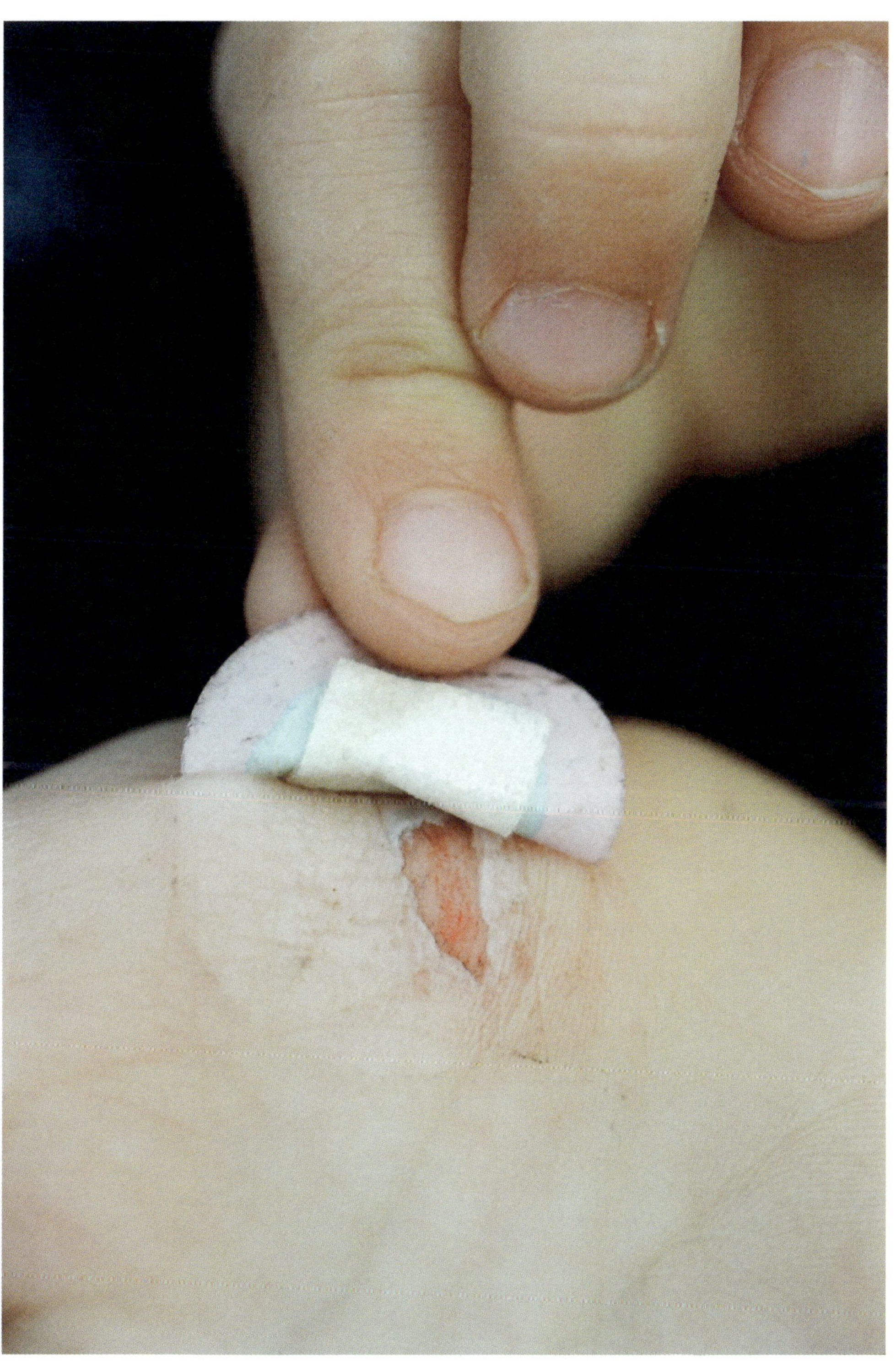

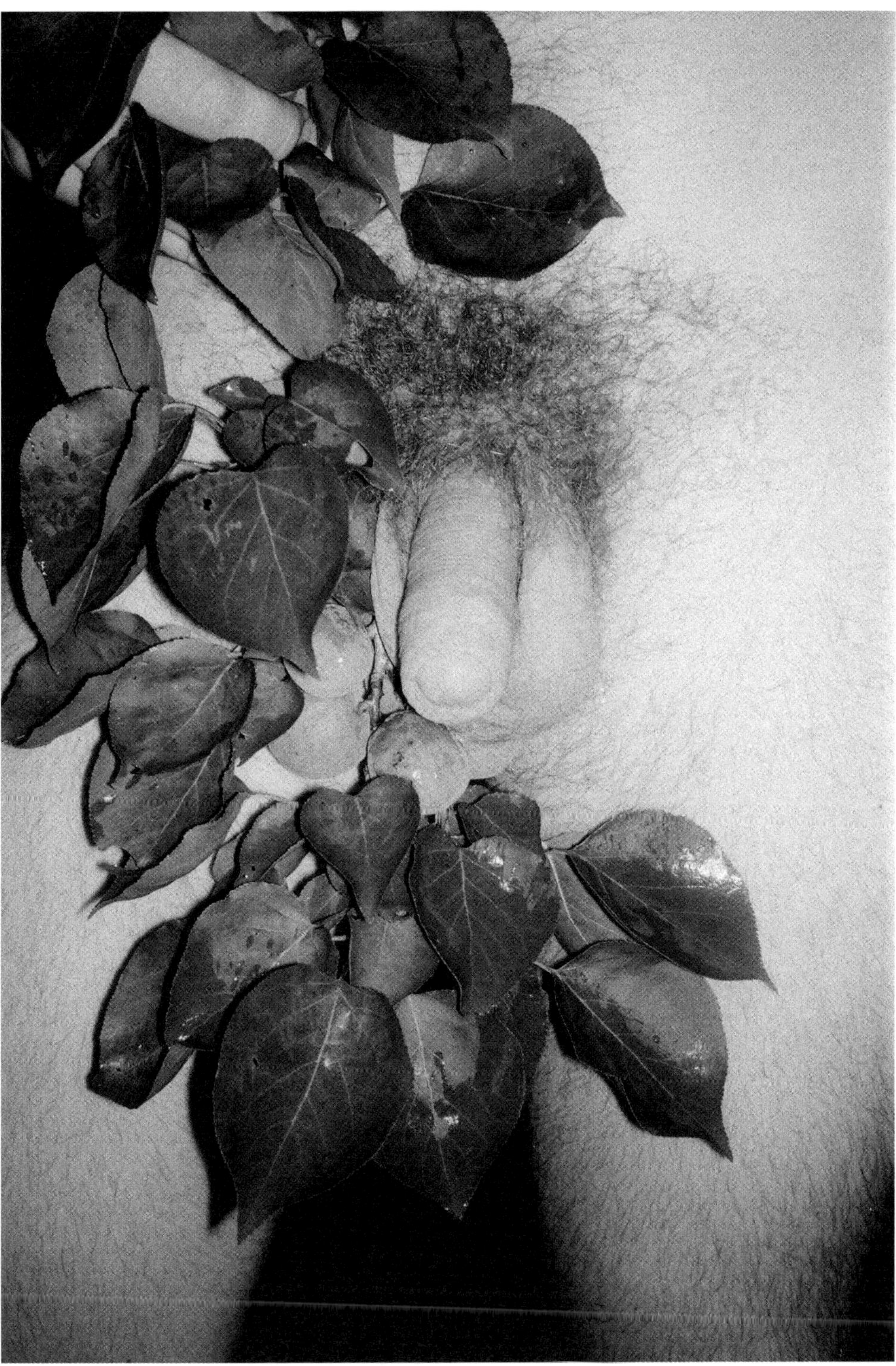

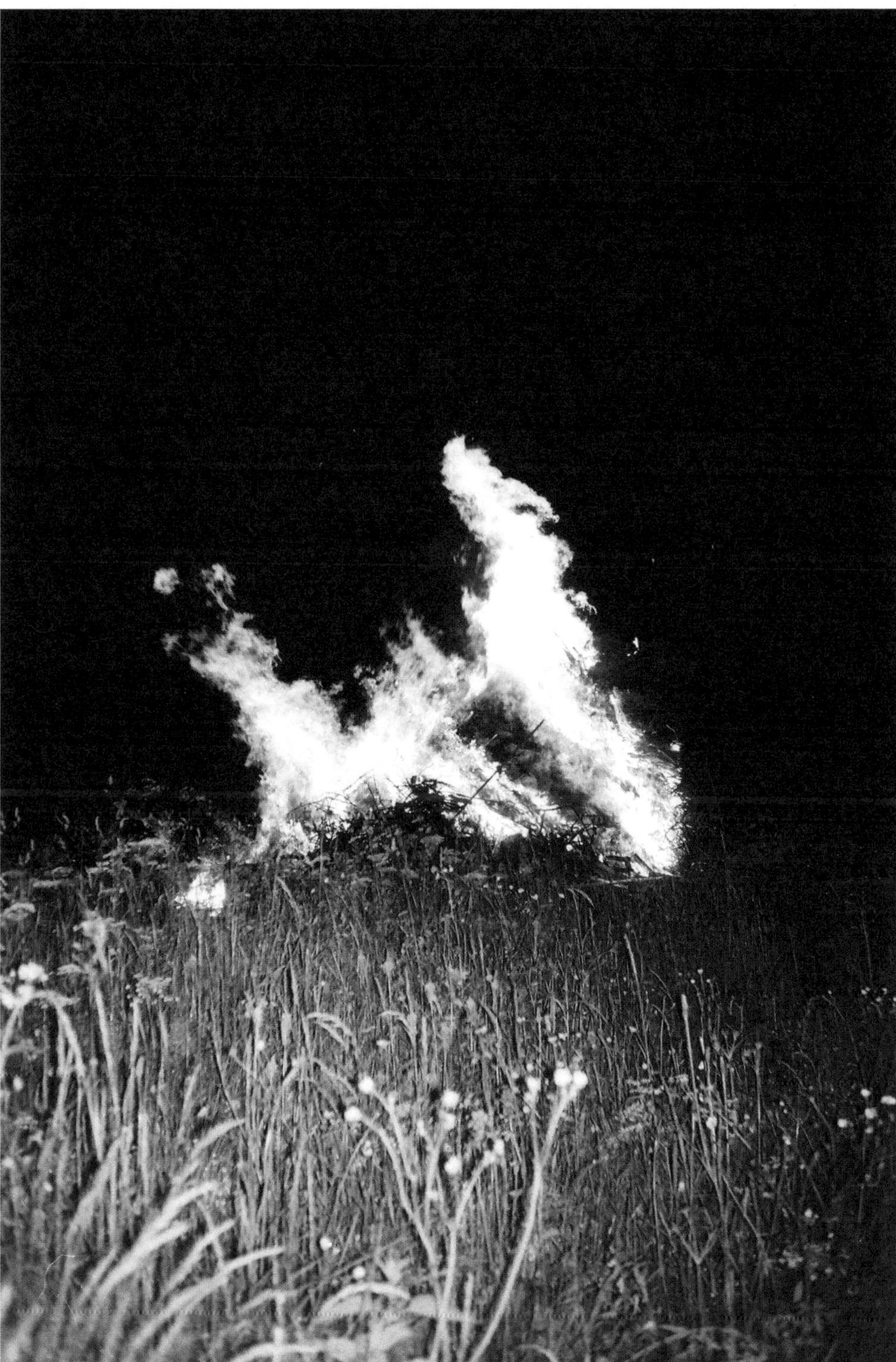

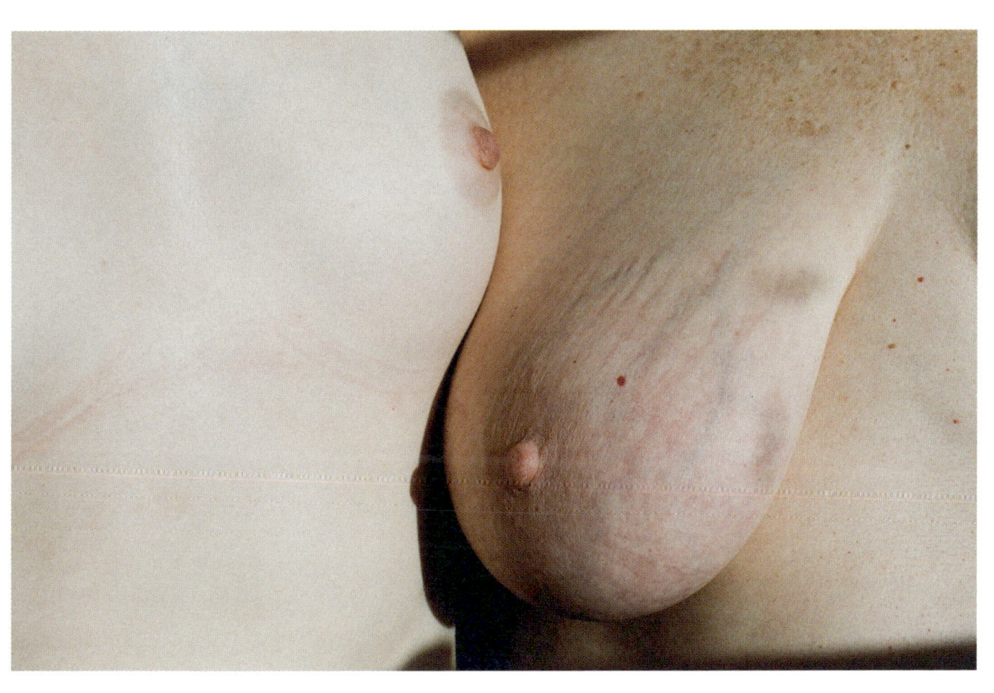

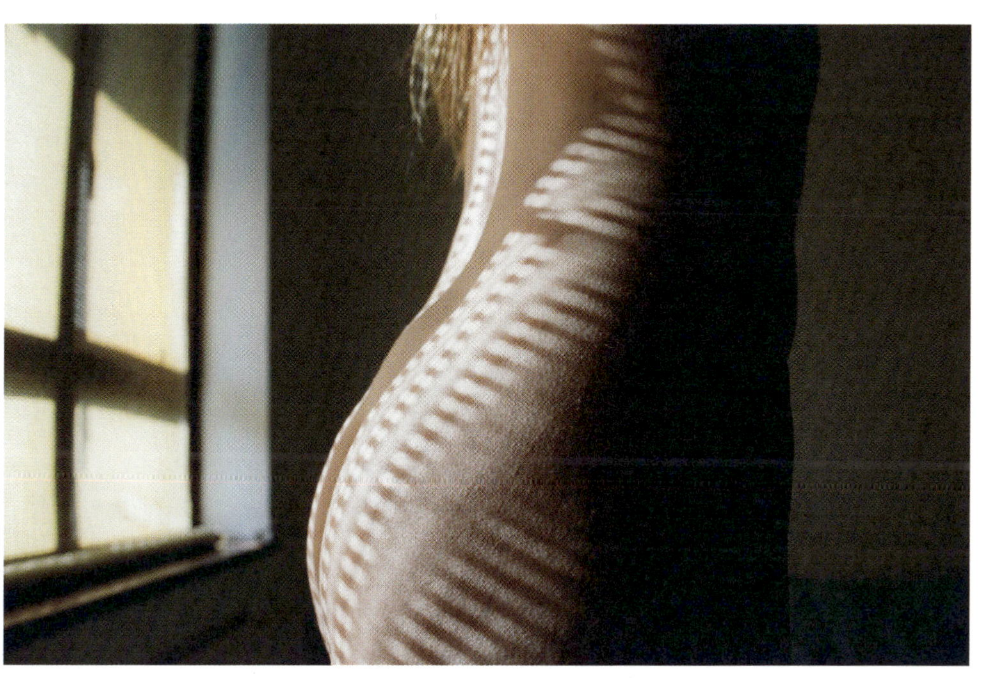

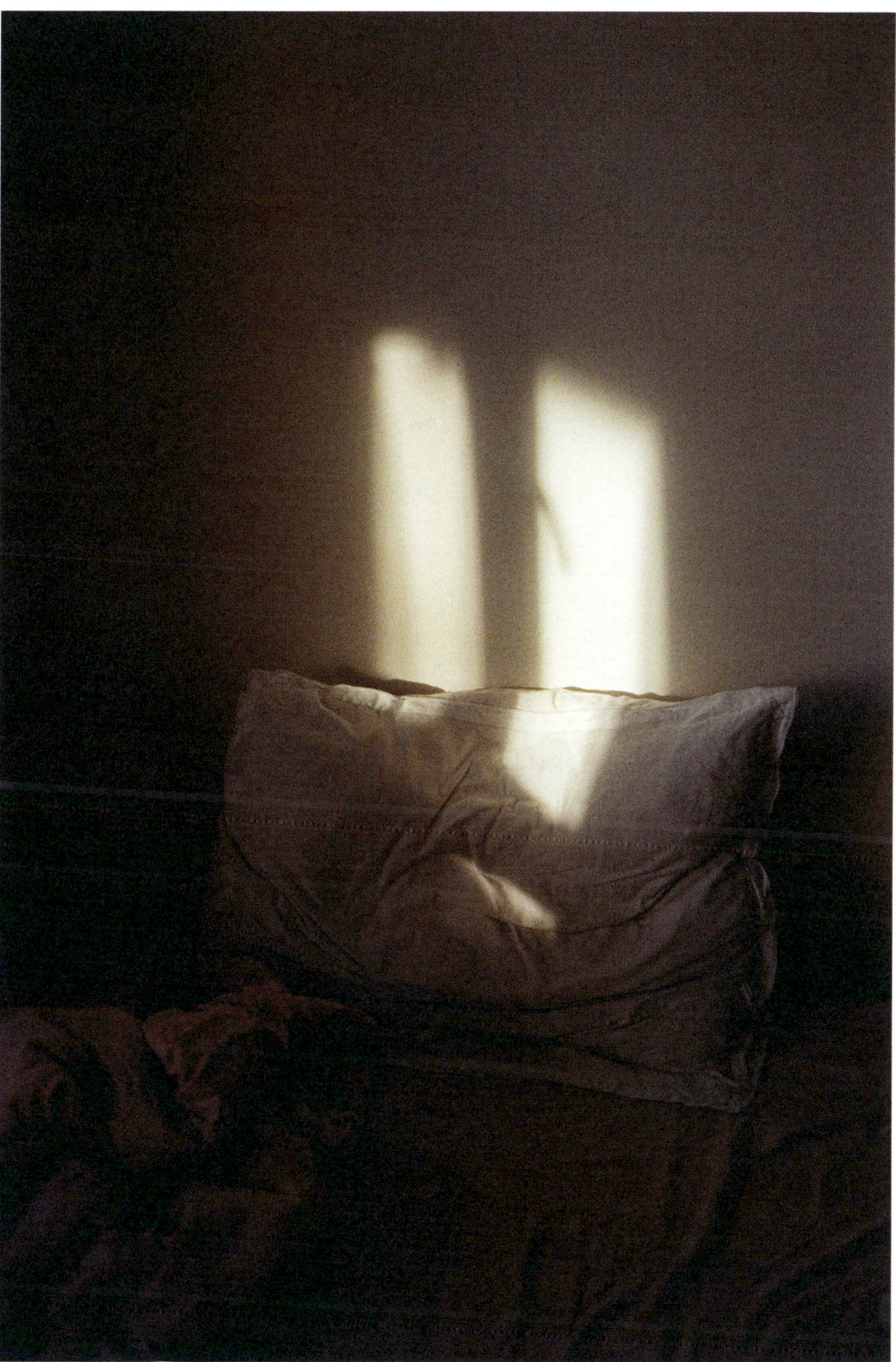

12

by Lina Scheynius
All photographs taken between 2017 and 2019
Thanks to Adrienne, Amanda, Aron, Carl, Étienne, Hanna,
Marina, Marvin, Ruby, Viktoria

First edition of 1000
Published in November 2023
by David Desrimais, Lina Scheynius and Emma Zampieri

Legal deposit: December 2023
ISBN 978-2-36568-080-6
Printed in Lithuania

JBE Books
90 rue de la Folie-Méricourt
75011 Paris
jbe-books.com